Endorsements

Gold Mines of Glory is a timely and uplifting work that calls believers to a deeper walk marked by discipline, purpose, and spiritual clarity. Pastor Ejaz Nabie leads readers toward the kind of success that honors God and strengthens the soul. His words gently remind us that when we order our steps according to God's design, He empowers us to rise to every calling. This book will encourage your faith and guide you toward a life shaped by God's favor and blessing.
—**Tim Hill**, Former General Overseer, Church of God

My dear friend, Rev. Ejaz, carries a wealth of wisdom shaped by both life and ministry. *Gold Mines of Glory* is a powerful collection of principles that, when applied, can cultivate meaningful growth and propel your life forward.
—**Rev. Steve Millazo**, Senior Pastor, Bethlehem AOG, President – Hope Day Network, Valley Stream, NY

Pastor Ejaz Nabie provides us with a wealth of visionary insight into the heart of God. This is a fantastic contribution of devotional thought.
—**Dr. Mac Pier**, Founder, Movement.org

With pastoral sensitivity and theological clarity, Pastor Nabie offers a compelling vision of Christian maturity. *Gold Mines of Glory* combines thoughtful exegesis, practical application, and spiritual depth for laypeople and enriching for scholars.
—**Dr. David Sobrepena**, Senior Pastor, Word of Hope, General Superintendent AOG, Manila Philippines

Ejaz Nabie's book, *Gold Mines of Glory*, is just that. It's a gold mine full of golden nuggets of wisdom, revelation, and a lifetime of acquired knowledge that he is sharing with us. I can't decide which chapter is my favorite because they're all so good. All I can say is WOW!
—**Gary Brothers**, Pastor of Discover Life Church, President of Vision of Hope International

If you're longing for a voice that cuts through the clutter and calls you upward, this is that voice. *Gold Mines of Glory* is not another devotional to skim but a treasure map to live by. Pastor Nabie writes with the steadiness of a seasoned shepherd and the sharp discernment of a spiritual strategist. His words don't just inspire—they orient, anchor, and awaken.

This book is rich with lived wisdom, biblical depth, and practical guidance that actually works in the grit of daily life. Page after page, Pastor Ejaz calls us into holy intentionality, Jesus identity, costly integrity, steadfast industry, Spirit-fueled innovativeness, and world-blessing impact that outlasts the moment and outlives the motions of the emotions.

These are not just gold nuggets—they are gold mines. Dig deep.
—**Leonard Sweet**, Prolific Author, Professor, Preacher, Publisher, Proprietor

The pages of this book are like threads that connect one gold mine of well-organized information on specific issues to the next.

This book, *Gold Mines of Glory*, is a source of significant profit and an invaluable resource for discipleship in advancing God's Kingdom. Read and be blessed.
—**Rev. Dr. Desmond Austin**, President of the Trinidad and Tobago Council of Evangelical Churches, Senior Pastor of the Tunapuna Open Bible Church

GOLD MINES of GLORY

100 Gold Nuggets *for* Peace & Prosperity in Your Life

Ejaz Nabie
Foreword by Dr. James O. Davis

Orlando, Florida

Copyright © 2026 by Ejaz Nabie

Gold Mines of Glory

Printed in the United States of America

ISBN: 979-8-9855197-4-7

All rights reserved. No part of this document may be reproduced or transmitted in any form, by any means (electronic, photocopying, recording, or otherwise) without the written permission of the author.

Unless otherwise indicated, Bible quotations are taken from the Holy Bible, New International Version®, NIV® Copyright ©1973, 1978, 1984, 2011 by Biblica, Inc.® Used by permission. All rights reserved worldwide.

Other Bible versions used:

Scripture marked (NKJV) is taken from the New King James Version®. Copyright © 1982 by Thomas Nelson. Used by permission. All rights reserved.

The ESV® Bible (The Holy Bible, English Standard Version®), © 2001 by Crossway, a publishing ministry of Good News Publishers. ESV Text Edition: 2025.

King James Version (KJV). Public Domain.

New American Standard Bible 1995 (NASB1995). New American Standard Bible®, Copyright © 1960, 1971, 1977, 1995 by The Lockman Foundation. All rights reserved.

Holy Bible, New Living Translation (NLT). Copyright © 1996, 2004, 2015 by Tyndale House Foundation. Used by permission of Tyndale House Publishers, Inc., Carol Stream, Illinois 60188. All rights reserved.

Amplified Bible, Classic Edition (AMPC). Copyright © 1954, 1958, 1962, 1964, 1965, 1987 by The Lockman Foundation.

Cover by Debbie Lewis

Billion Soul Publishing
Orlando, Florida
www.billionsoulpub.com

Dedication

To my beloved wife, **Sandra**,
and my cherished granddaughters, **Mia** and **Lana**—
you are my constant inspiration.
Your love and light reflect the grace of God in my life.

Contents

Foreword xi
Introduction xv

The Discovery of Gold Nuggets in Your Life 1

1 "According to Your Faith" 3
2 Confronting the Sin of Racism 5
3 Worry Can't Add 7
4 "Do You Want to Be Healed?" 9
5 The Spirit of a Finisher 11
6 Becoming a Safe Person 13
7 The Power of Hope 15
8 Facing Your Giants 17
9 Leading with a Divine Anointing 19
10 The Truth We All Know 21
11 Three Keys to Real Peace 23
12 What You Focus on Develops 25
13 The Only Answer to Offense 27
14 Preparing a Place for Heaven to Land 29
15 You're Not Old – Until Passion Dies 31
16 Attracting Momentum Through Hope 33
17 When Time and Intention Run Out 35
18 The Vulnerability of the Called 37
19 Born With Purpose, Equipped by God 39
20 Say Yes to the Bigger Dream 41
21 Lead Yourself First 43
22 When Thoughts Become Words 45
23 God's Answer to Chaos 47
24 Winning the Battle of the Mind 49
25 Rebounding from Crisis at Ziklag 51

The Digging for Gold Nuggets for Your Life 53

26 Living Ready 55
27 The Power of Relationships 58
28 Lay Aside Every Weight 61

29	Breaking Free from Deception	63
30	Freedom from the Voice of Accusation	66
31	"How Can This Be?"	68
32	Praying for Your Children	70
33	The Habit of Prayer	72
34	Living a Prayer-Filled, Purpose-Driven Life	74
35	Blessed to Multiply	76
36	The Blessing That Flows Through Generations	78
37	Speak, Lord – I'm Listening	80
38	Living Ready, Serving Well	82
39	The Power of Remaining	85
40	A Blessed Nation Begins with a Praying Church	87
41	Walking on Level Ground	89
42	Eyes That See More	91
43	The Gift of Perfect Peace	93
44	The God of All Comfort	95
45	A Life That Commands Respect	97
46	Devoted to Prayer, Driven by Purpose	100
47	Priorities in Ministry	102
48	Let Your Light Shine	104
49	Living for His Glory	107
50	Kingdom-Minded Leadership	110

The Development of Gold Nuggets Through Your Life 113

51	Passing the Baton of Faith	115
52	Why We Give	118
53	Created with Purpose and Destiny	121
54	The Rhythm of Prayerful Living	123
55	The God of Second Chances: Peter's Story	126
56	Training for Godliness	128
57	Victory Over Fiery Darts	131
58	Breaking Spiritual Bondages	133
59	The Battle of a Doubtful Mind	136
60	The Power of Forgiveness	138
61	Walking in Freedom	140
62	Replacing Lies with Truth	142
63	The Mind of Christ	144

64	Overcoming Flesh Patterns	146
65	Steps to Freedom	148
66	Overcoming Temptation	150
67	Battlefield of the Mind	153
68	Healing the Wounds Within	155
69	Breaking My Alabaster Jar	157
70	Does God Still Heal?	159
71	Equipped to Serve	161
72	Abraham's Journey of Faith	163
73	When You're Not in the Right Place	165
74	The Key to Successful Daily Living	167
75	Joseph: A Quiet Man of Unshakable Character	170

The Display of 24-Karat Pure Gold in Your Life 173

76	Believing God for the Impossible	175
77	Living with Honor	177
78	When God Writes on the Wall	179
79	Living a Life of Significance	182
80	Who Is Controlling You?	184
81	You Have What You Tolerate	187
82	The Power of Resurrection Faith	189
83	When the Strong Feel Weak	191
84	A Journey of Surrender and Succession	193
85	Claiming the Promises	195
86	The Power of Grace Over Judgment	197
87	When God Says "Enough"	199
88	Where Is Your Treasure?	201
89	Faith, Obedience, and Generational Continuity	203
90	Sowing into God's Future	206
91	When Jesus Touches the Untouchable	208
92	Unlocking the Power of Unity	210
93	Growth Is a Kingdom Principle	213
94	Speak Life, Shape Destiny	216
95	A Life of Encouragement and Humility	219
96	When Life Feels Out of Control	221
97	Trusting God in Impossible Situations	223
98	God's Way to Make Decisions	226

99	God's Got You	229
100	Invest in Souls: The Eternal Value of a Life	231

Extra Gold Mine Nuggets to Enrich Your Life.................233

101	Begin with the End in Mind	235
102	Finding Strength in the Secret Place	237
103	Strength in the Storm	240
104	A Fresh Start	242
105	What Are You Willing to Give?	244
106	Freedom from the Trap of Offense	247
107	When People Try to Hurt You	249

A Final Word to the Reader 253

Foreword

By Dr. James O. Davis

Many years ago, the Spanish Armada of 1715 was sailing off the coast of Florida. A hurricane struck, and those ships that were laden with millions of dollars in gold and silver ingots went to the bottom, in shallow water. People knew the treasure had been lost, but they didn't know where the ships had gone down. One ship went down near Vero Beach, Florida.

No doubt, over the years thousands of people have been in that water, swimming, scuba diving, snorkeling, spear fishing, but they didn't come up with any millions. The ships were there in shallow water. Fisherman undoubtedly fished over that spot. They would hang a hook, perhaps, on a lump of gold, and curse their luck, because they had hung a hook down beneath the water on something they could not see.

Then one day, an explorer said, "The ship must be here." They went out, and they made the surveys. They tested and went down into the water. Then, there it was, in shallow water—so shallow that any of us who could swim could have gone to the bottom. They brought up millions of dollars. All along people did not know in the shallow waters were the treasures from a previous generation.

The Christian life is not so high that you can reach it; it's so low that you get down to it. An ordinary person, surrendered to the Lord, can understand how to live the victorious life. You don't have to have a PhD; you don't have to learn Greek and Hebrew to learn what we're going to learn in. Ejaz Nabie's latest book, *Gold Mines of Glory*, The Bible is such a wonderful book. It is shallow enough that a little child can come and get a drink without fear of drowning, and so deep that the scholars can swim in it and never touch bottom.

The apostle Paul writes about Jesus as "in whom are hidden all the treasures of wisdom and knowledge" (Colossians 2:3). All the treasure is in the Lord Jesus Christ. It's hidden in Christ. Why did

God hide it? So you and I could have the joy of discovering it. The treasure is available; it's all for us. Yet, what we must do is to discover and appropriate our treasure?

Years ago, there was a ship that was out in the ocean, off the coast of Brazil, and the ship was without water. The people on board the ship, though surrounded with water, were dying of thirst. They saw another ship, and they sent a message to the other ship by semaphore, and said, "Do you have any water? We need water." The other ship sent a message back, and said, "Let down your buckets where you are." They said, "No, you don't understand." They sent another message, "We need drinking water." They sent back the message again, "Let down your buckets where you are." They let down their buckets and came up with fresh water, because they were at the mouth of the mighty Amazon River! The fresh water of the Amazon River was flowing out into the ocean and bringing fresh water to where they were, while they thought they were dying of thirst and surrounded by water they couldn't drink. They failed to appropriate that which was all around them. I want to encourage you to let down your bucket and experience the reviving waters of Jesus Christ!

Ejaz Nabie is the senior pastor of Faith Assembly in Queens, New York, and executive producer of Global Church Network's Conferences and Summits. He and I have traveled the world together. We have prayed together, planned together, laughed together, and wept together. He is impeccable in his character and inspirational in his commitment. You hold in your hands the gold mines of glory. Ejaz Nabie has unearthed by faith in this life the eternal treasures for us. He has shown us where the trustworthy treasures are buried just beneath the surface of our consciousness and demonstrates personal applications for us to have victory.

If you knew you were only 365 steps away from finding all of the treasures of wisdom and knowledge, would you take the necessary steps to have all this treasure? If you knew you only needed to fill one bucket per day, in order to have an ocean of victory, would you do it?

Ejaz Nabie, in *Gold Mines of Glory*, has shown us the faith-filled steps and has handed us buckets filled with blessings. All we have to do is take one step per day and drink the living water offered to us. I am thrilled to know the author. I highly recommend with all the emotion of my soul this powerful life-saving resource to you. Let's find the hidden treasures of wisdom and knowledge in Christ!

—**Dr. James O. Davis**, Founder/President
Global Church Network
Global Church Divinity School
Cutting Edge International
GCNW.tv

Introduction

This book is the result of the gentle but persistent encouragement of my dear friend, Dr. James O. Davis. For several years, he urged me to gather my sermons and share them in written form. I finally decided to follow his wise counsel—transforming a selection of my sermons into easy-to-read devotionals that speak to both the heart and the mind.

When King Solomon wrote the Proverbs, he clearly stated the purpose of his writing:

"Their purpose is to teach people to live disciplined and successful lives, to help them do what is right, just, and fair" (Proverbs 1:3, NLT).

God's Word was never meant merely to inform us, but to transform us. The Proverbs remind us that true wisdom produces a life marked by discipline and success—though not the kind of success the world celebrates. Instead, it is the success that honors God, blesses others, and brings deep peace to the soul.

A *disciplined life* is one shaped by intentional choices rather than impulsive reactions. It means training our hearts and habits to align with God's truth, even when obedience is inconvenient or unpopular. A *successful life*, in God's eyes, is not measured by possessions, popularity, or power, but by faithfulness and fruitfulness.

Discipline is the bridge between desire and destiny.

Many people desire to grow, change, or make a difference—but without discipline, those desires eventually fade. When you commit to daily spiritual habits—prayer, studying Scripture, serving others, and living with integrity—God shapes your character and prepares you for greater purpose.

Every small act of discipline builds spiritual strength. Over time, that strength positions you to experience God's best—not because you've earned it, but because you've become ready to steward it well.

As Proverbs 12:1 reminds us:

"To learn, you must love discipline; it is stupid to hate correction" (NLT).

Discipline is the soil where divine success grows.

This book was written to help believers build their lives around spiritual rhythms that cultivate discipline and, ultimately, godly success.

May each page bless you, challenge you, and inspire you to live the disciplined and successful life that brings glory to God.

The Discovery of Gold Nuggets in Your Life

1

"According to Your Faith"

"Then he touched their eyes and said, 'According to your faith let it be done to you'" (Matthew 9:29, NIV).

Jesus' words in Matthew 9:29 are simple yet profound: "According to your faith let it be done to you." Faith is more than belief—it's expectation. It is an inner attitude that shapes what we receive from God. How you think about God—whether He is able, willing, and faithful—will either open the door to His blessings or hold you back in fear and doubt.

The battle is often won or lost in the mind. What are you expecting from God today? Are you anticipating His favor, His help, His healing, and His guidance? Or have doubt and fear limited your vision? What you expect is often what you receive—this is the law of expectation. Faith activates the promises of God.

Look at David in 1 Samuel 17. When he faced Goliath, he didn't waver. His words and attitude showed unwavering confidence in God. He expected victory—and that expectation:

- **Honored God.** David believed God was bigger than the giant.
- **Increased his ability.** Confidence empowered his action.
- **Encouraged others.** His faith stirred courage in fearful soldiers.

If David had walked into the battle thinking, *I hope I make it*, he likely wouldn't have. But faith changed everything.

Let this shape how you live today:

- Start your day with faith, not doubt. "In the morning, Lord, you hear my voice; in the morning I lay my requests before you and wait expectantly" (Psalm 5:3).
- Look for something good in everyone and everything. Expect God to work in all circumstances.
- Watch your words. "Do not let any unwholesome talk come out of your mouths, but only what is helpful . . ." (Ephesians 4:29).
- Surround yourself with people of faith. Stay close to those who lift you up and avoid chronic complainers who drain your hope.
- Thank God in advance. "Have faith in God . . . Whatever you ask for in prayer, believe that you have received it, and it will be yours" (Mark 11:22–24).

REFLECTION

1. **Faith Determines Your Experience with God** – What are you expecting to receive from Him?
2. **Expectation Honors God** – Are you trusting His power and goodness to bring Him glory?
3. **Faith Influences Others** – How does you confidence in God inspire and influence others?

PRAYER

Lord, help me live today in faith. Let my thoughts, words, and expectations line up with Your promises. Strengthen my heart to believe that You are able to do more than I can ask or imagine. I expect the best because You are the best. In Jesus' name. Amen.

2

Confronting the Sin of Racism

"From one man he made all the nations, that they should inhabit the whole earth; and he marked out their appointed times in history and the boundaries of their lands" (Acts 17:26).

"Anyone who claims to be in the light but hates a brother or sister is still in the darkness" (1 John 2:9).

Racism is not merely a cultural issue or a social wound—it is a spiritual matter that grieves the heart of God. At its core, racism contradicts the truth of God's creation and the message of the Gospel. It distorts identity, divides humanity, and dishonors the image of God in every person.

1. RACISM IS BUILT ON REDUCTION

At the heart of racism is the idea that one group must devalue another in order to elevate itself. This is rooted in pride, fear, and insecurity—not truth.

But in the Kingdom of God, there is no room for reduction—only reconciliation and restoration.

"Do nothing out of selfish ambition or vain conceit. Rather, in humility value others above yourselves" (Philippians 2:3).

2. RACISM QUESTIONS THE CHARACTER OF GOD

To suggest that God made one race superior is to say that God is partial, biased, and unjust. But Scripture clearly tells us that God shows no favoritism (Romans 2:11). He made every human being in His image—equal in worth, value, and dignity.

God does not create hierarchy based on color, culture, or country—He creates unity through Christ.

3. RACISM HINDERS GOD'S WORK

Where there is racism, there is division. Where there is division, there is resistance to the Spirit of God. Racism damages the witness of the Church and blocks people from serving and encountering God. It keeps the body of Christ fragmented, ineffective, and unloving.

We cannot claim to love God and despise His creation.

"Whoever claims to love God yet hates a brother or sister is a liar" (1 John 4:20).

REFLECTION

Ask yourself today:

1. Am I harboring prejudice in my heart, whether subtle or overt?
2. Do I value people who look or live differently than I do?
3. Am I standing up for unity and justice, or staying silent in the face of division?

Racism is a sin to repent of, not just a problem to discuss. God is calling His Church to walk in truth, love, and justice—embracing the full beauty of His diverse creation.

PRAYER

Father, I acknowledge that racism is a sin against You and Your image in others. Search my heart and reveal any prejudice within me. Help me to see others as You see them. Heal our land, purify Your Church, and let us be instruments of unity, love, and truth. In Jesus' name. Amen.

3

Worry Can't Add

"And which of you by worrying can add one cubit to his stature?" (Luke 12:25, NKJV).

In this verse, Jesus asks a piercing question: What does worry accomplish? His point is simple yet profound—worry doesn't make us taller, healthier, or more secure. It's powerless to change the future but powerful in stealing our peace.

In biblical terms, a "cubit" was a measurement of about 18 inches, often used to describe the length of a forearm. By saying you can't "add one cubit" to your height (or "one hour" to your life, as some translations read), Jesus exposes the futility of anxiety.

Worry feels productive because it keeps our minds busy. But in truth, it's like running on a treadmill—you expend energy but go nowhere. Jesus points us to a better way: instead of letting our minds loop on fear, we shift our gaze to the God who provides.

This teaching sits within Jesus' broader call in Matthew 6 and Luke 12: "Do not worry about your life . . . Look at the birds . . . See the flowers . . ." These everyday images remind us that God's creation flourishes without anxiety—because it's sustained by His care.

Worry says: "It's all up to me."

Faith says: "My Father knows and will provide."

This doesn't mean we avoid planning or responsibility—it means we refuse to live under the illusion that anxiety controls outcomes. Instead, we acknowledge that peace comes from entrusting tomorrow to the One who already holds it.

REFLECTION

Ask yourself today:

1. What situation in your life do you find yourself constantly worrying about?

Write it down and beside it, list what you can do in faith and then what you must leave in God's hands.

PRAYER

Father, You know my needs before I even speak them. Forgive me for the times I cling to worry as if it could change my situation. Teach me to trust You with both the details and the unknowns of my life. Help me shift my energy from anxious thoughts to faithful action, and let my heart rest in the truth that You are my provider. In Jesus' name. Amen.

4

"Do You Want to Be Healed?"

"When Jesus saw him lying there and learned that he had been in this condition for a long time, he asked him, 'Do you want to get well?'" (John 5:6).

At the Pool of Bethesda, Jesus made a deliberate choice. He chose to be there. He chose to notice one man out of the crowd. And He chose to engage someone who had been sick for 38 years. But even with Jesus standing in front of him, healing didn't just happen automatically.

Jesus asked a surprising question: "Do you want to get well?"

It may seem obvious. Who wouldn't want to be healed? But Jesus didn't assume. The man had to make a decision—he had to choose healing.

Why ask such a question? Because healing isn't just about ability; it's about willingness. Some people, like the man at the pool, may be so used to their pain, dysfunction, or brokenness that change actually feels threatening.

There are real reasons why people choose not to be healed:

- **Comfort in the familiar.** After 38 years, lying down had become his lifestyle.
- **Loss of sympathy or attention.** He may have feared becoming invisible if he was no longer a beggar.
- **Fear of responsibility.** Healing meant working, contributing, and no longer depending on others.
- **Emotional barriers.** Sometimes people isolate themselves through pain, using it as a shield.
- **Past trauma.** Like some women who've endured abuse, choosing bitterness or self-protection can feel safer than

choosing healing. But in doing so, they keep the abuser's control alive, day after day.
- **The illusion of safety in pain.** For many, staying stuck is easier than facing the uncertainty of change.

But Jesus still asks today: "Do you want to be made well?"
Not can you, but do you.

Healing begins with a choice. Jesus is present, willing, and able—but He won't override your will. You have to want freedom more than familiarity. You have to choose to break the cycle, to release the past, to forgive, to let go, to get up.

REFLECTION

1. What have you been lying beside for too long?
2. Is there a wound, a habit, a relationship, or a mindset that's kept you from wholeness?
3. Jesus is near. He's asking you today—not just offering healing, but inviting your response:
4. "Do you want to be healed?"

PRAYER

Lord Jesus, You see me as I am—every hidden wound, every fear, every place I've settled beside the pool of my own pain. Thank You that You draw near, not to condemn but to restore. Today, I choose to say *yes* to Your question. Yes, I want to be healed. Give me the courage to rise from what's familiar, to let go of excuses, and to walk in the wholeness You offer. Heal not only my body, but my mind, my heart, and my memories. Teach me to trust Your goodness more than my comfort, and Your promise more than my pain. Amen.

5

The Spirit of a Finisher

"Now finish the work, so that your eager willingness to do it may be matched by your completion of it" (2 Corinthians 8:11).

In a world obsessed with fast results and instant gratification, it's easy to start strong and finish weak. But God calls us to be finishers—to follow through, endure the process, and complete the work He's entrusted to us. Just like Noah, who built the ark over many decades without seeing a single drop of rain, we are called to press forward even when the end seems far off or unclear.

Noah didn't just have faith—he had faith that finished. His obedience preserved his family, fulfilled God's plan, and impacted the world. If he had stopped halfway, he would have forfeited his destiny. The same is true for us. Whether it's a calling, a relationship, a goal, or a healing journey—quitting is not an option.

To develop the spirit of a finisher, we must embrace four vital qualities:

1. PATIENCE

"Let us not become weary in doing good, for at the proper time we will reap a harvest if we do not give up" (Galatians 6:9).

Patience reminds us that God's timing is perfect. Though we may not see immediate results, we trust that He is working behind the scenes.

2. PERSEVERANCE

"Let us run with perseverance the race marked out for us . . ." (Hebrews 12:1–3).

Finishing well requires us to press through setbacks, opposition, and discouragement. Jesus endured the cross with the joy set before Him—we too must keep our eyes fixed on Him.

3. DETERMINATION

"Now finish the work . . ." (2 Corinthians 8:11).

Determination bridges the gap between desire and completion. It moves us from intention to action. Many are eager to begin, but only the determined reach the end.

4. DISCIPLINE

"No discipline seems pleasant at the time . . . but it produces a harvest . . ." (Hebrews 12:11).

Discipline means doing what needs to be done, even when we don't feel like it. It's the muscle that carries us through the mundane and the difficult.

REFLECTION

1. Where in your life have you started something with passion but now feel weary or uncertain?
2. Have you let time, opposition, or delay discourage your progress?

God's promise still stands: if you don't give up, you will reap. Keep showing up. Keep building. Keep trusting.

PRAYER

Lord, give me the heart of a finisher. Strengthen me with patience when things move slowly, perseverance when I feel discouraged, determination when I feel like quitting, and discipline when the journey gets tough. Help me to complete what You've called me to do and bring glory to You through my faithfulness. In Jesus' name. Amen.

6

Becoming a Safe Person

"Let love be genuine. Abhor what is evil; hold fast to what is good" (Romans 12:9, ESV).

In a world filled with judgment, betrayal, and broken trust, people long for safe places and safe people—those who reflect God's character in how they love, listen, and live. Becoming a safe person is not about being perfect; it's about being trustworthy, stable, and Christ-centered in our relationships. Safe people help others grow, not shrink. They create space for healing, not harm.

Here are five biblical traits that help us become the kind of person others feel safe with:

1. LIVE TO GLORIFY GOD, NOT PLEASE PEOPLE

"Am I now trying to win the approval of human beings, or of God? . . . If I were still trying to please people, I would not be a servant of Christ" (Galatians 1:10).

A safe person is led by God, not driven by the opinions of others. People-pleasers are inconsistent, manipulative, and often insecure. But God-pleasers seek truth and love above popularity. They love honestly, not to impress but to glorify God.

2. CELEBRATE OTHERS' SUCCESS

"Rejoice with those who rejoice; mourn with those who mourn" (Romans 12:15).

A safe person is not threatened by others' victories. Do you rejoice in others' growth, or secretly feel better when they fail? Philippians 4:8 reminds us to think on things that are true, noble, right, pure, lovely, and admirable. A safe heart finds joy in others' success.

3. REFUSE TO CONTROL OTHERS

Love doesn't manipulate. Safe people don't use guilt, fear, or pressure to get their way. They respect boundaries, allow freedom, and trust God to work in others. Control is a counterfeit form of love—but trust is its true expression.

4. HONOR CONFIDENTIALITY

"A gossip betrays a confidence, but a trustworthy person keeps a secret" (Proverbs 11:13).

Safe people don't leak what was shared in confidence. They understand the weight of trust and guard it. Confidentiality is not about hiding truth but protecting hearts.

5. BE A GENUINE FRIEND

"A friend loves at all times, and a brother is born for a time of adversity" (Proverbs 17:17).

Genuine friendship is loyal, not seasonal. It shows up in hardship, stays when others leave, and offers grace when others judge. A safe person sticks closer than a brother (Proverbs 18:24).

REFLECTION

1. Am I someone others feel safe around?
2. Do my words heal or harm?
3. Do people see Jesus in how I listen, love, and respond?

Being a safe person is a daily decision—to love like Christ, speak with integrity, and stay faithful through every season.

PRAYER

Father, make me a safe person. Purify my heart from the need to please people. Help me to celebrate others, respect boundaries, keep confidences, and be a friend who loves like You. Let my life reflect the safety of Your presence. In Jesus' name. Amen.

7

The Power of Hope

"Why, my soul, are you downcast? Why so disturbed within me? Put your hope in God, for I will yet praise him, my Savior and my God" (Psalm 42:11).

1. WHAT IS HOPE?

Hope is the confident expectation of good—rooted not in circumstances, but in God's character and promises. It is the anchor of the soul (Hebrews 6:19), holding us steady through the storms of life. Hope is the inner assurance that no matter how dark the night, morning is coming. It's not wishful thinking—it's a firm trust that God is still writing your story, and the best is yet to come.

Hope lifts your eyes off the present pain and fastens them on God's unchanging goodness.

It says, "God is not finished. Something better is ahead."

2. WHAT CAUSES HOPE TO DIE?

Hope doesn't vanish suddenly—it fades slowly, drained by:
- Unmet expectations – When what we prayed for doesn't happen.
- Long delays – "Hope deferred makes the heart sick . . ." (Proverbs 13:12).
- Loss and grief – When life changes without warning.
- Repeated failure – When we feel stuck or too broken to begin again.
- Voices of negativity – When others speak doubt, fear, and discouragement.

Hope dies when we stop looking up and start believing the lie that things will never change.

3. WHAT HAPPENS WHEN HOPE DIES?

"Take from a person his wealth, and you hinder him; take from him his purpose, and you slow him down. But take from him his hope, and you stop him" (Unknown).

Hope is like oxygen for the soul. Without it, we don't just lose motivation—we lose life. When hope dies:

- Dreams fade.
- Joy disappears.
- Faith weakens.
- Despair creeps in.
- Spiritual paralysis takes hold.

A person can live for a while without money. They can press forward without clarity of purpose. But without hope, they give up. Despair suffocates. Depression overtakes. Life becomes empty and heavy.

4. BUT THERE IS STILL HOPE

The good news is this: Hope can be restored.

He specializes in breathing life into dead things—dreams, hearts, and futures. No matter how broken or discouraged you feel today, hope is not lost. Jesus is alive, and that means your story isn't over.

REFLECTION

1. Have you lost hope in a dream, a relationship, or your purpose?
2. Have the delays, disappointments, or pain convinced you that it's over?

Lift your eyes. Put your hope in God. He hasn't left you. He hasn't forgotten you. And He is still the God who makes all things new.

PRAYER

Father, I admit there are places in my heart where hope has died. I've grown weary, discouraged, and even numb. But I turn to You—the source of true hope. Breathe life into me again. Restore what has been lost, and remind me that Your plans for me are still good. I put my hope in You, and I choose to praise You—no matter what. In Jesus' name. Amen.

8

Facing Your Giants

"Then David said to the Philistine, 'You come against me with sword and spear and javelin, but I come against you in the name of the LORD Almighty . . . All those gathered here will know that it is not by sword or spear that the Lord saves; for the battle is the LORD's'" (1 Samuel 17:45, 47).

We all face giants—obstacles that seem bigger than our strength, louder than our courage, and stronger than our will. Giants come in many forms: fear, insecurity, debt, illness, rejection, addiction, or even past failures. Like Goliath, they taunt us, try to define us, and demand our retreat.

But like David, we are not called to run in fear—we are called to face our giants with faith. Here's how:

1. UNDERSTAND WHAT OR WHO IS YOUR GIANT

Before you can defeat your giant, you must name it. David knew Goliath wasn't just a man—he represented fear, intimidation, and defiance against God's people.

What is your Goliath?

Be honest. Identify it. Giants lose power when exposed by truth.

2. STRATEGIZE YOUR MOVE / PLAN YOUR ACTION

David didn't charge Goliath blindly—he approached with purpose. He chose five smooth stones and came in confidence.

Facing your giant requires wisdom and a spiritual strategy.

Pray. Plan. Get counsel. Take action, not just emotion.

3. GLEAN FROM YOUR EXPERIENCE

David remembered the lion and the bear. He didn't forget what God had already brought him through. Your past victories are reminders that God has been faithful before—and He will be again.

Your history with God fuels your courage today.

4. USE WHAT GOD HAS GIVEN YOU

Saul offered David his armor, but David couldn't wear what didn't fit. Instead, he used a sling and stones—tools he was familiar with.

Don't envy others' weapons. Use your voice, your gift, your story, your prayer life. What God has given you is enough.

5. REMEMBER THE BATTLE IS THE LORD'S

David didn't win because he was skilled—he won because he trusted God. The battle wasn't about his strength, but God's power.

When you face your giant in God's name, you never fight alone. Victory is promised—not because you're strong, but because He is.

REFLECTION

1. What giant is standing in front of you today, daring you to back down?
2. What would it look like to face it with faith instead of fear?

God isn't asking you to fight in your own power—He's asking you to trust Him, move forward, and believe that the victory belongs to Him.

PRAYER

Lord, help me to face the giants in my life with courage and faith. Show me what I'm really up against, give me a plan, and help me to trust You fully. Remind me of the battles You've already won in my life. I choose to use what You've given me, and I stand in the confidence that the battle is not mine—it's Yours. In Jesus' name. Amen.

9

Leading with a Divine Anointing

"Then the LORD came down in the cloud and stood there with him and proclaimed his name, the LORD" (Exodus 34:5).

When Moses descended from Mount Sinai carrying the new tablets of the Law, something extraordinary happened—his face shone with the glory of God. The Israelites couldn't ignore it. Moses wasn't just carrying commandments; he was carrying the presence and anointing of God.

That divine glow was more than a physical sign—it symbolized the power and presence of God resting on a leader. Moses had spent time with God, and it showed. His leadership was not rooted in position or personality, but in anointing.

So what does it mean to be an anointed leader today? Can others sense God's presence in your life and leadership? The devotional from Exodus 34:5–7 offers four marks of divinely anointed leadership:

1. CHARISMA – A GIFTED PRESENCE

"The anointed enjoy a sense of giftedness that comes from God" (John Maxwell).

This isn't about charm or showmanship—it's about a spiritual magnetism that draws others to Christ in you. When you lead with charisma from God, people feel safe, inspired, and seen.

2. CHARACTER – GOD'S NATURE WITHIN YOU

People see God's nature in your leadership. They trust you.

Anointed leadership reflects God's heart. It's marked by integrity, humility, and trustworthiness. People follow character, not just skill—because it gives them confidence in who you are when no one is watching.

3. COMPETENCE – EFFECTIVE LEADERSHIP

You have the ability to get the job done. Your leadership produces results.

Anointed leaders don't just inspire—they deliver. God equips those He calls. When you're walking in your divine assignment, your effectiveness is not based on natural strength alone but on supernatural ability.

4. CONVICTION – COURAGE TO STAND FIRM

"Your leadership has backbone. You always stand for what is right."

Anointed leaders are not swayed by pressure or popularity. They lead with courage, speaking truth in love and choosing righteousness over comfort. They don't bend when it matters most.

REFLECTION

1. Are you leading from your own strength, or from God's anointing?
2. Do people see Christ in your words, your work, and your walk?

Like Moses, you can't lead well until you've been in the presence of God. Let His glory shape you before you go out and lead others.

PRAYER

Lord, anoint me to lead with Your presence. Let my leadership reflect Your charisma, character, competence, and conviction. May I not rely on my own strength, but on Your Spirit. Help me walk closely with You, so that others may see You in me. In Jesus' name. Amen.

10

The Truth We All Know

"So God created mankind in his own image, in the image of God he created them; male and female he created them" (Genesis 1:27).

In a world filled with questions about identity, purpose, and value, three powerful and foundational truths—three absolutes—stand firm. These truths apply to every person, in every culture, at every time in history. They speak to the dignity, brokenness, and longing that define the human condition.

1. EVERY HUMAN IS MADE IN THE IMAGE OF GOD

You were not created by accident or randomness. You were formed by God, in His image, with divine intent. That means you have worth, beauty, purpose, and potential.

No matter what your past, status, or story—you reflect something of the Creator.

To bear God's image is to have value that cannot be erased.

When we understand this truth, it changes how we see ourselves and how we treat others. Every person—friend or stranger, strong or weak—is stamped with the image of God.

2. EVERY IMAGE IS DISTORTED BY SIN

Though we are made in God's image, we are not what we were meant to be. Sin has marred the reflection. We lie, we hurt, we rebel, we fear. The world is broken, and so are we. The image is still there—but it's smudged, twisted, and faded by sin.

We feel the gap between who we are and who we were made to be.

But there is good news: Christ came not only to save us but to restore the image of God within us. In Jesus, the distorted can be redeemed, and the broken can be made whole.

3. EVERY HUMAN KNOWS THERE'S SOMETHING MORE

Deep in every heart is a quiet ache—a restless sense that this world isn't enough.

We know, somehow, that we were made for more than just survival, more than pain, more than emptiness. That's not weakness—it's awareness.

Hope stirs in the soul because eternity is written on our hearts (Ecclesiastes 3:11).

This longing points us back to God. It is a holy clue that He exists, and He desires to fill what nothing else can satisfy. We chase success, relationships, or comfort—but only God can meet the longing He Himself placed in us.

REFLECTION

1. Do you see yourself and others through the lens of God's image, God's grace, and God's glory?
2. Are you willing to let Him restore what sin has distorted?
3. And are you responding to the longing not with distraction, but with pursuit of His presence?

PRAYER

Father, thank You that I am made in Your image. I confess that sin has distorted what You designed, but I believe you sent Jesus to restore it. Teach me to see myself and others through Your eyes. Fill the longing in my heart with Your truth, Your presence, and Your love. I was made for more—and I find that "more" in You. In Jesus' name. Amen.

11

Three Keys to Real Peace

"Peace I leave with you; my peace I give you. I do not give to you as the world gives. Do not let your hearts be troubled and do not be afraid" (John 14:27).

In a world full of stress, uncertainty, and fear, many search for peace but come up empty. Real peace isn't the absence of problems—it's the presence of God. It's a steady heart in a shaking world, anchored not in circumstances but in truth.

Someone once said the three keys to real peace are:
- Fret not.
- Faint not.
- Fear not.

These aren't empty phrases—they are powerful truths grounded in God's Word.

1. FRET NOT – BECAUSE GOD LOVES YOU

"And so we know and rely on the love God has for us. God is love" (1 John 4:16).

When life gets overwhelming, it's easy to worry, overthink, and spiral into anxiety. But God says, "Don't fret—I love you."

His love is not passive; it's powerful, personal, and ever present.

When you rest in His love, fear loses its grip. You are fully known and fully loved—and that changes everything.

2. FAINT NOT – BECAUSE GOD HOLDS YOU

"Even there your hand will guide me, your right hand will hold me fast" (Psalm 139:10).

In moments of weakness, weariness, or discouragement, it's tempting to give up. But God says, "Don't faint—I'm holding you."

Even when you feel like you're falling apart, His hand is strong and steady.

You don't have to carry life alone. God is guiding, sustaining, and upholding you—even when you can't see it.

3. FEAR NOT – BECAUSE GOD KEEPS YOU

"The LORD watches over you—the LORD is your shade at your right hand" (Psalm 121:5).

Fear tries to paralyze you with what-ifs and worst-case scenarios. But God says, "Don't fear—I'm watching over you."

You are not exposed to life's chaos. God is your protector, your covering, your keeper.

He is closer than you think, guarding your steps and calming your fears.

REFLECTION

1. Are you fretting today? Feeling faint? Gripped by fear?

Let God's love calm your worry, His hand lift your weakness, and His presence silence your fear. Peace isn't something you chase—it's someone you trust.

PRAYER

Lord, I confess I often fret, faint, and fear. But today, I choose to rest in Your love, rely on Your hand, and trust in Your protection. Thank You for holding me, guiding me, and keeping me in perfect peace. I put my heart in Your hands. In Jesus' name. Amen.

12

What You Focus on Develops

"Set your minds on things above, not on earthly thing." (Colossians 3:2).

A simple principle of photography offers us profound spiritual insight: Whatever you focus on always develops.

When you point a camera lens at something and adjust the focus, that subject becomes sharp and clear, while everything else fades into the background. It's not that other things aren't there—they're just not your focus.

In the same way, your life follows your focus.

What you give your attention to begins to grow. What you think about shapes your attitude. What you dwell on determines your direction. Whether it's fear or faith, pain or purpose, chaos or Christ—what you magnify will multiply.

1. CONSIDER THIS

- Are you constantly focusing on what's going wrong?
- Do you replay past hurts or future fears?
- Or are you choosing to center your heart on God's promises?

There may be many things happening around you—distractions, noise, pressure—but what you lock your spiritual lens on will shape how you see everything else. Focus on God's faithfulness, and you'll find peace. Focus on His Word, and you'll grow in truth. Focus on Jesus, and you'll walk in purpose.

2. PHILIPPIANS 4:8 REMINDS US:

"Whatever is true, whatever is noble, whatever is right, whatever is pure, whatever is lovely, whatever is admirable—if anything is excellent or praiseworthy—think about such things."

In other words: Focus your mind on what matters.

Let your thoughts develop into faith, your vision sharpen around truth, and your life reflect the clarity that comes from fixing your eyes on Jesus.

REFLECTION

1. What have you been focusing on lately—worries, offenses, failures, or God's goodness, grace, and guidance?

What you focus on develops. Choose today to focus your spiritual lens on the One who never changes.

PRAYER

Lord, help me to fix my focus on You. With so many distractions around me, I confess I've often let fear, doubt, and negativity fill my view. But today, I choose to center my heart on Your truth, Your promises, and Your presence. Let what develops in me be faith, peace, and purpose. In Jesus' name. Amen.

13

The Only Answer to Offense

"Bear with each other and forgive one another if any of you has a grievance against someone. Forgive as the Lord forgave you" (Colossians 3:13).

Offense is a wound—sometimes small, sometimes deep. But no matter how it comes, if it's left unresolved, it doesn't just sit quietly in the background. It lingers, festers, and waits for a moment to erupt.

Like an unhealed infection, offense will beg for a way out—through anger, bitterness, sarcasm, withdrawal, or even revenge. It doesn't disappear on its own. It demands an answer.

And there is only one: Forgiveness.

1. WHY FORGIVENESS?

Because it's the only response that brings peace instead of poison.

It's not letting someone "off the hook"; it's taking the hook out of your own heart. Forgiveness doesn't mean you deny the hurt—it means you refuse to let the hurt define you.

It means you give to God what only He can judge and heal.

2. IF YOU DON'T FORGIVE...

- The offense will grow roots of bitterness.
- Your heart will become hardened, and your spirit, restless.
- You'll find yourself replaying the offense, waiting for the perfect moment to unleash it—on the offender or even to someone who had nothing to do with it.

You weren't made to carry offense. That weight will break you. But forgiveness? It frees you.

3. JESUS UNDERSTANDS

Jesus endured the ultimate offense: betrayal, mockery, abuse, and crucifixion. Yet hanging on the cross, He said, "Father, forgive them . . ." (Luke 23:34).

Why? Because He knew forgiveness was the only path to healing—for them and for us.

REFLECTION

1. Is there an offense sitting inside you—waiting to be expressed through anger, distance, or silence?

Today, give it to God. Choose forgiveness. Not because the person deserves it, but because you deserve freedom.

PRAYER

Father, I confess there are wounds I've held onto—offenses that have lived in my heart too long. I don't want to carry them anymore. Today, I choose to forgive. Help me release the pain to You. Heal what's broken and give me the strength to live in the freedom of Your grace. In Jesus' name. Amen.

14

Preparing a Place for Heaven to Land

"Your kingdom come, your will be done, on earth as it is in heaven" (Matthew 6:10).

When God desires to bring a slice of heaven to earth, He doesn't drop it randomly from the skies. He looks for a place to land, a heart, a life, a people ready to carry His glory and reveal His will. Just like a plane needs a runway, heaven needs a landing place.

And so, God anoints and appoints ordinary people to prepare sacred ground. That means you.

1. GOD NEEDS A PREPARED PEOPLE

Throughout Scripture, whenever God moved mightily on earth, He first prepared someone:

- Noah built an ark.
- Moses led a nation.
- Mary carried the Messiah.
- John prepared the way.
- The early Church received the Spirit.

In every case, God found someone willing to be a vessel, someone who said, "Here I am, Lord." He still looks for that today—not for perfect people, but available ones.

2. WHAT DOES IT MEAN TO PREPARE A LANDING PLACE?

- **Consecrate Your Heart.** Make room for God in your thoughts, desires, and decisions.
- **Cultivate Obedience.** Heaven lands where people say "yes" to God's will, even when it's costly or inconvenient.

- **Create Atmosphere.** Worship, prayer, purity, and unity are like spiritual landing lights that invite God's presence.
- **Be Expectant.** Believe that God wants to use you to bring healing, peace, love, and power into the lives around you.

3. YOU ARE GOD'S CHOSEN GROUND

Heaven doesn't always land in cathedrals—it lands in classrooms, kitchens, offices, neighborhoods, wherever a surrendered heart says, "Lord, use me." You are the runway God wants to build on, light up, and launch from.

REFLECTION

1. Are you preparing a place in your life for heaven to land?
2. Have you given God full access to use your time, words, and gifts to bring His presence into the world around you?

PRAYER

Father, I want to be a place where heaven touches earth. Anoint me and appoint me to prepare the way for Your Kingdom in my life, my family, and my community. Cleanse my heart, strengthen my spirit, and let Your will be done through me. I say yes—make me a landing place for Your glory. In Jesus' name. Amen.

15

You're Not Old – Until Passion Dies

"Even to your old age and gray hairs I am He, I am He who will sustain you. I have made you and I will carry you; I will sustain you and I will rescue you" (Isaiah 46:4).

We often define age by numbers—how many years we've lived, how much we've accomplished, or how many candles sit on our birthday cakes. But true age isn't marked by time, it's marked by passion.

You aren't really old until you've outlived your passion.

When your heart no longer burns for purpose . . .

When your soul no longer leans toward growth . . .

When your spirit no longer reaches for more of God—that's when age settles in.

1. PASSION IS THE FLAME OF PURPOSE

God never created us to simply exist. He wired us for calling, pursuit, and impact. Whether you're 25 or 85, as long as you're breathing, God still has something for you to do, to learn, and to love.

Think of Moses, who didn't start leading until age 80. Or Caleb, who said at 85, "Give me this mountain!" (Joshua 14:12). Or Anna the prophetess, who spent her later years worshiping and praying in the temple, preparing hearts for Jesus' arrival.

Passion isn't a season, it's a choice.

It's what happens when we stay connected to God, fueled by His Word, and stirred by His Spirit.

2. WHEN PASSION FADES, LIFE SHRINKS

Without passion, life becomes small. We settle. We coast. We talk more about what was than what could be. But God never intended for our fire to go out. He calls us to live with eyes lifted, hearts ignited, and faithfully engaged.

You can grow old without ever growing cold.

3. KEEP YOUR FLAME ALIVE

- Stay curious – keep learning, asking, growing.
- Stay connected – surround yourself with people who stir your spirit.
- Stay committed – keep saying yes to God, even when it's hard.
- Stay in love – with Jesus, with people, with the calling on your life.

REFLECTION

1. Have you allowed passion to fade?
2. Are you living off memories of past fire, or is your heart still burning for what God can do today?

PRAYER

Lord, reignite my passion. Don't let me settle into comfort, routine, or passivity. Remind me that age is not a barrier to purpose. As long as I have breath, give me the fire to love You deeply, serve You faithfully, and live with holy ambition. In Jesus' name. Amen.

16

Attracting Momentum Through Hope

"May the God of hope fill you with all joy and peace as you trust in him, so that you may overflow with hope by the power of the Holy Spirit" (Romans 15:13).

Momentum is a powerful force. When it's working for you, it feels like doors open, favor follows, and progress is natural. But when momentum is lost—through failure, discouragement, or disappointment, it can feel like everything stalls.

Here's the truth:

You attract momentum when you replace failure and disappointment with hope and energy.

Hope isn't naïve. It's not pretending things didn't go wrong. Hope is a spiritual decision to believe that God still has more, even after a setback. It's the ability to shake off the dust and say, "I'm not done yet."

1. DISAPPOINTMENT DRAINS. HOPE REFUELS.

Disappointment, when left unchecked, creates a toxic environment. It:

- Drains passion.
- Clouds perspective.
- Paralyzes movement.

But hope breathes life into the room. When you choose to believe again, you:

- Create space for growth.
- Draw in the energy of faith.
- Build an environment where God can move.

You don't have to fix everything at once. Just take one step, one prayer, one renewed thought—and momentum will start building again.

2. YOU CREATE WHAT YOU CULTIVATE

Momentum is often a byproduct of the atmosphere you set. When you cultivate:

- Hope over despair.
- Gratitude over grumbling.
- Action over apathy.

You create a space where things begin to flourish. People are drawn to your energy. Ideas come. Strength rises. The Holy Spirit empowers. That's how momentum returns.

REFLECTION

1. Have you been sitting in disappointment or failure too long?
2. What would shift if you chose hope and brought fresh energy to your situation—even if it's small?

You may be one hopeful choice away from momentum returning.

PRAYER

Lord, I give You every place of failure and disappointment. I don't want to live stuck or drained. Fill me with Your hope and renew my energy. Help me create an atmosphere of faith and movement in my life. I believe You still have more for me, and I'm choosing to step forward again. In Jesus' name. Amen.

17

When Time and Intention Run Out

"There is a time for everything, and a season for every activity under the heavens" (Ecclesiastes 3:1).

Life is full of both moments and motives—some things run out of time, while others run out of intention. And both require our attention if we want to live wisely and walk faithfully.

1. SOME THINGS RUN OUT OF TIME

Not every door stays open forever.

Opportunities expire. Seasons shift. People move on. God sometimes closes one chapter so another can begin. If we're not paying attention, we may mourn what ended instead of stepping into what's next.

There's grace in knowing that God works through seasons, and we don't have to cling to what has passed. When something runs out of time, it's not always failure; it may simply be fulfillment. Ask: Is this over because I missed it, or because its purpose is complete?

2. SOME THINGS RUN OUT OF INTENTION

We start things with great vision—relationships, ministries, habits, goals—but slowly, intention fades. Passion cools. Purpose gets buried under routine or distraction. What once had life becomes stale—not because time ran out, but because we stopped being intentional.

What are you still doing outwardly that no longer has inward commitment?

Are you drifting in areas where you once were driven?

Sometimes, revival doesn't mean something new; it may mean renewed intention in what already exists.

3. GOD REDEEMS BOTH

Whether something has run out of time, or lost its intention, God is not caught off guard.

- If time has ended, He can give you a new season.
- If intention has faded, He can reignite the fire.

Either way, His grace meets you right where you are.

REFLECTION

1. What in your life has run out of time?
2. What needs renewed intention?

Ask the Holy Spirit for wisdom to know the difference—and courage to respond in obedience.

PRAYER

Lord, help me discern what in my life is ending because its time is up, and what needs the revival of my intention. Give me the grace to let go when You're closing a door, and the discipline to reignite what You've called me to carry. I trust that every season and every motive is in Your hands. In Jesus' name. Amen.

18

The Vulnerability of the Called

"It is God who arms me with strength and keeps my way secure" (Psalm 18:32).

The call of God is a sacred assignment—a divine pull toward purpose. But with that call comes vulnerability. It doesn't make you invincible; in fact, it often exposes your deepest weaknesses.

When you carry a divine promise, you also carry pressure—to fulfill it, to protect it, to explain it. And like Abraham and Sarah, you may find that the greatest threat to your calling isn't the enemy out there, but the tension within.

1. VULNERABLE TO THE FLESH

God gave Abraham and Sarah a promise: a son. But as time passed and the promise was delayed, they leaned into their flesh—their own reasoning, their own solution. The result? Ishmael.

When we become impatient, we often birth things God never intended—relationships, decisions, platforms, plans that may look good but are not God. Ishmael wasn't just a child—he became a rival to the promise.

What you produce in the flesh may later mock what God wanted to do by the Spirit.

2. VULNERABLE TO TIMING

There's a burden that comes with waiting. Delay can make you question if you heard God right. And when you're vulnerable to time, you're tempted to act out of urgency instead of obedience.

You rush ahead of God, trying to make it happen in your own strength. But every promise of God comes with a divine timetable, and trusting Him means trusting His clock, not yours.

3. VULNERABLE TO PEOPLE

When God's promise seems slow or silent, you start listening to other voices. You become man-conscious—worried about opinions, perceptions, and pressures.

You start asking:

- What will they think if I don't succeed?
- Should I do more to make this look like it's working?
- Maybe they're right . . . maybe I missed it.

But the call of God can't be measured by the approval of people. Man didn't call you—God did.

4. THE GOOD NEWS

Even when Abraham and Sarah made a mistake, God didn't cancel the promise. He still brought forth Isaac—the true child of destiny.

Your vulnerability doesn't disqualify you—it reminds you to stay dependent on God.

REFLECTION

1. Where have you grown vulnerable in your calling?
2. Are you striving in the flesh, rushing God's timing, or overly focused on people's opinions?

Let God remind you: He will fulfill His promise. Stay faithful. Stay dependent. Stay surrendered.

PRAYER

Lord, thank You for calling me. I confess I've grown vulnerable—to fear, to pressure, to my own timing. Forgive me for any "Ishmaels" I've birthed in impatience. Help me to wait with faith, walk in step with Your Spirit, and ignore the noise of man's opinion. I trust You to finish what You started in me. In Jesus' name. Amen.

19

Born With Purpose, Equipped by God

"Before I formed you in the womb I knew you, before you were born I set you apart; I appointed you as a prophet to the nations" (Jeremiah 1:5).

God's first words to Jeremiah are astounding—not just for what they say, but how they are said: in the past tense.

"Before I formed you . . . I knew you . . . I set you apart . . . I appointed you."

Before Jeremiah ever spoke a word, took a breath, or felt a calling, God already had a plan.

1. YOUR PURPOSE WAS SETTLED BEFORE YOU WERE BORN

God didn't wait to see how Jeremiah turned out before deciding his purpose—He declared it from the beginning.

And the same is true for you.

You are not an accident. You were appointed, not improvised.

Until Jeremiah saw why he was born, he didn't understand what he was capable of.

You will never know what you can do until you know why you were born.

2. PURPOSE UNLOCKS ABILITY

When Jeremiah heard his purpose, he resisted—he felt too young, too unqualified (Jeremiah 1:6). But God answered him in verse 9:

"Then the LORD reached out his hand and touched my mouth and said to me, 'I have put my words in your mouth.'"

Whatever God calls for, He provides.

God will never call you to do something He hasn't already given you the ability to do.

He doesn't need your self-confidence; He asks for your obedience. Your purpose determines your abilities, not the other way around.

3. YOU LIVE IN A NO-EXCUSE ZONE

In Christ, you are fully equipped for every assignment heaven has placed on your life.

- Not because you're perfect,
- Not because you feel ready,
- But because God empowers what He ordains.

There are no excuses—just opportunities to trust.

If God called you, you can do it—because He's doing it through you.

REFLECTION

1. Are you waiting to "feel ready" before you step into what God has spoken over your life?
2. Have you allowed excuses to silence your calling?

Ask God to remind you today that your purpose was decided before your birth, and He has already given you everything you need to walk it out.

PRAYER

Father, thank You for knowing me, calling me, and equipping me. Help me to stop waiting for confidence and start walking in calling. Silence my excuses. Open my eyes to see that if You have called me, You have also prepared me. I trust that my purpose is secure in You. In Jesus' name. Amen.

20

Say Yes to the Bigger Dream

"Now to him who is able to do immeasurably more than all we ask or imagine, according to his power that is at work within us" (Ephesians 3:20).

God is not limited by your résumé. He doesn't measure dreams by degrees or callings by credentials. God will always give you dreams bigger than your education. Why? Because He wants you to trust His power, not your preparation.

When God gives a dream or vision, it's never to frustrate you—it's to elevate you. He uses vision to call you out of average and into excellence.

1. GOD CALLS YOU TO COME OUT

Throughout Scripture, we see a consistent pattern: God calls people out before He brings them in.

- "Abraham, come out" – from your country to a land I will show you.
- "Moses, come out" – from the wilderness to lead My people.
- "David, come out" – from the field to the throne.

God always moves people from comfort to calling, from small thinking to Kingdom vision. And He's still doing it today.

2. THE POWER IS IN YOUR YES

You don't have to know how it will happen, you just need to say yes.

Nehemiah was a cupbearer, not a builder. He had no blueprint, no budget, and no obvious experience. But he had a burden. And when he said yes to that burden and spoke his vision, doors opened.

Nehemiah stood before the king and articulated what God had put in his heart. The moment he did, God moved. The king released resources, favor, and protection.

The provision followed the vision. The ability followed the obedience.

3. GOD ISN'T ASKING FOR YOUR PERFECTION— JUST YOUR PERMISSION

He doesn't call the qualified; He qualifies the called. And He's not asking you to figure it all out—just to step out. The dream God gave you is bigger than you because He wants to do it through you.

REFLECTION

1. What dream has God placed in your heart that seems bigger than your ability?
2. Have you said yes, or are you still waiting until you "feel ready"?

Remember—God is not calling you based on what you know, but based on who He is.

PRAYER

Lord, thank You for dreaming bigger for me than I dream for myself. I confess I've let fear, qualifications, or doubt hold me back. Today, I say yes. I step out of average and into purpose. I trust that as I move, You will provide everything I need. Use me to do what only You can do through me. In Jesus' name. Amen.

21

Lead Yourself First

"Apply your heart to instruction and your ears to words of knowledge" (Proverbs 23:12).

Leadership isn't just about influencing others—it starts with mastering yourself. Before you can effectively guide anyone else, you must learn to lead the person staring back at you in the mirror. And the first area to bring under leadership is your mind.

Your thoughts shape your choices. Your choices shape your habits. And your habits shape your life. That's why Proverbs 23:12 says,

"Apply your heart to instruction and your ears to words of knowledge."

In other words: Take responsibility for what you let in and what you think about.

1. YOU ARE THE FIRST PERSON YOU MUST LEAD

No one follows a leader who's lost within. You can't give directions if you don't have it yourself.

If you don't lead yourself in discipline, others won't follow your example.

If you don't manage your emotions, your leadership will be unstable.

If you don't set spiritual priorities, you'll lead from pressure instead of purpose.

Self-leadership is the foundation of godly influence.

Before God gives you more to lead, He teaches you how to lead yourself.

2. THE MIND IS THE FIRST ORGAN TO MASTER

Everything begins in the mind—faith, fear, peace, or panic. What you feed your mind determines your outlook and outcome. That's why Scripture urges us to renew our minds (Romans 12:2) and take every thought captive (2 Corinthians 10:5).

Your mind must be guarded, trained, and filled with God's truth daily.

You can't lead with clarity if your mind is cloudy with lies, distractions, or toxic thoughts.

3. APPLY AND ALIGN

Proverbs 23:12 tells us to apply our heart and tune our ears to wisdom. This takes intentionality. Leading yourself is not passive, it's a daily decision to:

- Set your mind on things above (Colossians 3:2).
- Speak truth over feelings.
- Guard your input (what you read, hear, and watch).
- Align your actions with God's Word.

REFLECTION

1. Are you leading yourself well?
2. What thoughts are you allowing to shape your direction today?
3. Have you taken control of your mind—or are your thoughts running wild?

PRAYER

Lord, help me lead myself first. Teach me to take ownership of my thoughts, my habits, and my choices. I surrender my mind to You—renew it, purify it, and align it with Your Word. Let me be a leader who leads from a place of self-discipline and spiritual clarity. In Jesus' name. Amen.

22

When Thoughts Become Words

"For as he thinks in his heart, so is he" (Proverbs 23:7, KJV).

Thoughts are never just thoughts. They are seeds planted deep in the heart that, if left unchecked, eventually break forth into words—and words shape your world.

You may think your thoughts are private, but they are silently shaping your perspective, your emotions, and eventually, your speech. As Proverbs 23:7 teaches us, what you consistently think, you become—and what you become, you eventually speak.

1. THOUGHTS ARE THE ROOT, WORDS ARE THE FRUIT

Jesus said, "Out of the abundance of the heart the mouth speaks" (Luke 6:45).

In other words, your tongue tells on your mind.

- If your thoughts are full of fear, your words will sound anxious.
- If your thoughts are bitter, your words will sting.
- If your thoughts are full of faith, your words will bring life.

That's why it's essential to guard your thoughts—because your words are simply your thoughts vocalized.

2. WORDS HAVE POWER

Proverbs 18:21 reminds us: "Death and life are in the power of the tongue."

But before they are in the tongue, they are in the mind.

If you want to change your speech, don't start with your mouth—start with your mind. Fill it with truth. Dwell on what is noble, pure, lovely, and praiseworthy (Philippians 4:8).

3. WHAT YOU THINK IN SECRET WILL BE SPOKEN IN PUBLIC

Eventually, what's internal becomes external. Thoughts leak. In a moment of stress or emotion, they break through the surface.

So be careful what you entertain in your thought life. You're not just "thinking"—you're shaping what you will one day say, and what you say affects everything around you.

REFLECTION

1. What thoughts are you nurturing today?
2. Are they aligned with God's truth or with fear, pride, or offense?
3. If those thoughts suddenly turned into words, would they bring life—or harm?

PRAYER

Lord, help me to guard my thoughts. Let my mind be a place where Your truth dwells richly, so that my words reflect Your heart. I don't want to speak carelessly or in ways that tear down. Fill me with wisdom and renew my thinking daily, so that what flows out of my mouth brings life and grace. In Jesus' name. Amen.

23

God's Answer to Chaos

"Now the earth was formless and empty, darkness was over the surface of the deep, and the Spirit of God was hovering over the waters" (Genesis 1:2).

Chaos has many faces—confusion, disorder, emotional unrest, broken relationships, and spiritual disarray. Whether it shows up in your family, your mind, your health, or your schedule, chaos is more than just inconvenience. It's the evidence of disorder where God's order is missing.

But the good news? The Holy Spirit brings order out of chaos.

1. THE SOURCES OF CHAOS

Chaos doesn't just appear out of nowhere. It has causes:
- Satan, who comes to steal, kill, and destroy (John 10:10).
- Disobedience to God, which opens doors to confusion.
- Selfish desires, when we are drawn away by our own lust (James 1:14).
- Ungodly habits or environments that erode peace.
- Broken systems in government, communities, or families.
- Health breakdowns that affect every area of life.
- Poor time management, leading to burnout and imbalance.
- An unwillingness to change, keeping us stuck in dysfunction.

Wherever chaos exists, it points to a need for divine intervention—and that's where the Holy Spirit comes in.

2. THE HOLY SPIRIT BRINGS ORDER

In Genesis 1, the earth was "formless and empty," covered in darkness and disorder. But the Spirit of God was hovering—not panicking, not confused. Hovering in readiness to act.

The first act of the Holy Spirit in Scripture was to bring order to chaos.

That is still His mission in your life today. When you invite Him in, He doesn't just soothe your feelings—He starts rearranging what's out of line:

- He brings clarity to confusion.
- He aligns your priorities.
- He corrects what's wrong and empowers what's right.
- He gives wisdom where you've felt lost.

3. INVITE GOD INTO THE CHAOS

You don't have to fix the chaos before God can move—you just have to invite Him in.

His presence brings peace. His voice silences the noise. His wisdom reveals what to keep, what to change, and what to surrender.

REFLECTION

1. Where in your life are you experiencing chaos right now?
2. Is it from spiritual neglect, poor decisions, or external circumstances?

Ask the Holy Spirit to hover over that area and begin restoring divine order.

PRAYER

Holy Spirit, I invite You into every chaotic place in my life. Where there is disorder, bring Your peace. Where there is confusion, speak clarity. Where I've contributed to chaos through disobedience or poor choices, forgive me and lead me in Your truth. Just as You brought order to the earth, bring order to my heart, my home, and my habits. In Jesus' name. Amen.

24

Winning the Battle of the Mind

"Those who live according to the flesh have their minds set on what the flesh desires; but those who live in accordance with the Spirit have their minds set on what the Spirit desires" (Romans 8:5).

If you want to win the battles of life, you must first win the battle of the mind.

You can't have a positive, purpose-filled, Spirit-led life with a negative, fearful, or undisciplined mind.

Where your mind goes, your life follows.

1. YOUR THOUGHTS BEAR FRUIT

Every thought is a seed, and seeds grow.
- A thought turns into a word,
- A word becomes an action,
- Actions become habits,
- And habits shape your future.

This is why Proverbs 18:21 says, "Death and life are in the power of the tongue,"—but those words begin as thoughts.

2. YOU MUST DECIDE WHERE TO SET YOUR MIND

Romans 8:5 makes it clear: we have a choice.

You can set your mind on the flesh (fear, lust, pride, negativity), or on the Spirit (truth, peace, righteousness, hope).

The direction of your life hinges on where you place your thoughts.

The mess of your life will not be straightened out until the mess of your mind is straightened out.

3. CHOOSE LIFE OVER DEATH

Deuteronomy 30:19 says, "I have set before you life and death . . . now choose life."

Every day, you get to choose what thoughts to entertain and what thoughts to reject. You are not a prisoner to your thoughts—you are a steward of them.

God has empowered you to choose:
- Faith over fear.
- Peace over panic.
- Forgiveness over bitterness.
- Truth over lies.

4. BRING EVERY THOUGHT INTO OBEDIENCE

Second Corinthians 10:5 urges us to "take every thought captive to make it obedient to Christ."

Not every thought deserves to live in your mind. You have to learn how to:
- Recognize the lie.
- Replace it with truth.
- Repeat truth until it renews your mind.

This isn't a one-time battle—it's a daily war. But it's a war you can win, because the Spirit of God lives in you.

REFLECTION

1. What thoughts have been unchecked in your mind lately?
2. Are they leading you closer to Christ—or further from peace and purpose?
3. What's one negative thought you can replace with God's truth today?

PRAYER

Lord, I surrender my mind to You. Help me to take every thought captive and make it obedient to Christ. I choose to set my mind on what the Spirit desires, not what my flesh wants. Train me to think in alignment with Your Word so I can live in victory. In Jesus' name. Amen.

25

Rebounding from Crisis at Ziklag

"But David found strength in the LORD his God" (1 Samuel 30:6).

Ziklag was David's lowest point. In 1 Samuel 30, we find David returning home only to discover his city burned and his people—his family—taken captive. Everything was gone. And what's worse, the very men who once followed him were ready to stone him.

David wasn't just facing loss—he was facing crisis.

1. WHEN THE ENEMY IS UNDERESTIMATED

Ziklag was attacked in David's absence.

We don't know if he took security for granted, but the outcome reminds us: When we take the enemy for granted, we risk the things that matter most.

- Verse 2: Their families were taken captive.
- Verse 4: The anguish was so deep, they wept until they had no strength left.

When we fail to stay spiritually alert, the enemy often strikes the most vulnerable places—our homes, our peace, our joy, our sense of security.

2. THE LONELINESS OF LEADERSHIP IN CRISIS

David's followers turned on him. He stood alone, grieving the same loss—but now also bearing blame.

Crisis has a way of isolating us. Even those closest may not understand what we carry.

But what David did next changed everything.

3. HOW DO YOU REBOUND FROM CRISIS?
David encouraged himself in the Lord (v. 6).
He didn't wait for someone else to lift him up—he went to God.
Self-encouragement isn't self-help—it's choosing to lean on God's strength when yours is gone.
David prayed (vv. 7–8).
Instead of acting out of panic, David paused to seek the Lord.
In crisis, prayer must come before pursuit.
David listened and obeyed.
God spoke: "Pursue, for you shall surely overtake and recover all."
The voice of God brought clarity, courage, and strategy.
David pursued the enemy.
He moved from pain to purpose. He didn't stay in sorrow—he acted in faith.
David recovered all (vv. 18–19).
What was lost was restored—not partially, but fully.
God doesn't just comfort in crisis—He can reverse the damage.

4. LESSONS FROM ZIKLAG
- The pain is real, but so is God's power to restore.
- Crisis will try to isolate you, but God will meet you in the silence.
- You can choose to encourage yourself, even when no one else will.
- Prayer brings direction, and direction leads to recovery.

REFLECTION
1. What crisis are you facing right now? What have you lost—peace, purpose, relationships, hope?
2. Have you paused to encourage yourself in the Lord and listen for His direction?

PRAYER

Lord, in times of crisis, I choose to turn to You. Strengthen me when I feel weak, and speak clearly when I feel lost. Help me to encourage myself in You, to pray with expectation, and to act with boldness. I believe that with You, nothing is permanently lost. Help me to recover what the enemy tried to steal. In Jesus' name. Amen.

The Digging for Gold Nuggets for Your Life

26

Living Ready

"Therefore, prepare your minds for action; be self-controlled; set your hope fully on the grace to be given you when Jesus Christ is revealed" (1 Peter 1:13).

Being ready is more than simply waiting. It means living with purpose, focus, and urgency—with eternity in mind. Jesus is returning, and Scripture repeatedly calls us to be ready, not distracted or spiritually dull.

To live ready is to live intentionally, valuing what God values and giving priority to what matters most.

1. PRIZE WHAT IS ETERNAL

What you value shapes how you live.

When you value eternal things, truth, holiness, souls, worship—you begin to let go of things that won't last.

"Set your minds on things above, not on earthly things" (Colossians 3:2).

2. SEEK TO BE UNTAINTED AND PURE

Living ready means pursuing holiness in a world that normalizes compromise.

We are not perfect, but we are called to be set apart—clean vessels for God's use.

"Everyone who has this hope in Him purifies himself, just as He is pure" (1 John 3:3).

3. AVOID STUMBLING—AND DON'T CAUSE OTHERS TO STUMBLE

Being ready also means walking wisely, mindful of how your actions impact others.

Your freedom should never be a stumbling block to another believer's growth.

"Be careful . . . that the exercise of your freedom does not become a stumbling block to the weak" (1 Corinthians 8:9).

4. BE SERIOUS AND WATCHFUL

In a world full of distractions, spiritual alertness is essential. We must not sleep spiritually while the world groans for truth.

"But the end of all things is at hand; therefore be serious and watchful in your prayers" (1 Peter 4:7).

5. DEMONSTRATE LOVE FOR FELLOW BELIEVERS

Loving others isn't optional—it's evidence that you belong to Christ.

True readiness is marked by genuine relationships, forgiveness, humility, and unity.

"By this everyone will know that you are my disciples, if you love one another" (John 13:35).

6. GIVE PRIORITY TO THE LORD'S WORK

Live each day as if it could be your last opportunity to serve Jesus.

Be faithful with your gifts, generous with your time, and eager to fulfill your purpose.

"Always give yourselves fully to the work of the Lord, because you know that your labor in the Lord is not in vain" (1 Corinthians 15:58).

REFLECTION

1. Are you living ready? Are your values, thoughts, relationships, and priorities aligned with eternity?
2. Ask yourself: If Jesus returned today, would I be found faithful, focused, and ready?

PRAYER

Lord, help me to live with a heart focused on eternity. Teach me to value what You value, to love purely, and to walk carefully. Let me not be distracted by the temporary but devoted fully to Your purpose. May I live ready—awake, watchful, and eager for Your return. In Jesus' name. Amen.

27

The Power of Relationships

"Do not be misled: 'Bad company corrupts good character'" (1 Corinthians 15:33).

Relationships shape everything. Your joy, your pain, your peace, your purpose are all deeply connected to who you allow into your life. The relationships you nurture today are the seeds of the future you will harvest tomorrow.

God created us for connection—but not every connection is divine. Some people are assignments from heaven . . . others are distractions or detours.

1. RELATIONSHIPS CAN MAKE OR BREAK YOU

Every relationship carries influence. It will either:
- Promote you toward your God-given destiny, or
- Demote you through compromise, distraction, or destruction.

"Your relationships will be your source of greatest joy or your avenue of greatest pain" (Stephen R. Covey).

The people closest to you affect your mindset, your emotions, your standards, and even your walk with God.

2. A SNAPSHOT OF YOUR FUTURE

Look around you. The people in your present are a preview of your future.

If they don't challenge you, sharpen you, or call you higher, they may be chaining you to a lower version of yourself.

3. A RELATIONSHIP QUIZ FOR THE SOUL

Take time today to reflect honestly:

- What unpleasant things are you tolerating right now because of a relationship you're in?
- Are you accepting anything now you once said you'd never allow?
- Has your conscience been dulled? Are there things that used to repulse you but now no longer do, because of someone's influence?
- Have your spiritual standards shifted downward due to someone's negativity, compromise, or pressure?

If the answers convict you, don't ignore it. That's the Holy Spirit inviting you to reassess your connections.

4. WISDOM IN CHOOSING PEOPLE

Jesus loved everyone, but He didn't walk closely with everyone. He chose His inner circle wisely. So should you.

Not everyone deserves access to your emotions, your energy, or your purpose.

5. SURROUND YOURSELF WITH LIFE-GIVERS

God sends people of purpose to walk with you, challenge you, pray for you, and hold you accountable. These relationships sharpen you, uplift you, and draw you closer to Christ.

"Walk with the wise and become wise, for a companion of fools suffers harm" (Proverbs 13:20).

REFLECTION

1. Are the people around you helping you become more like Christ—or less?
2. Do your current relationships elevate your standards or lower them?

Ask God for the discernment to know who to keep close and the courage to step back from unhealthy connections.

PRAYER

Father, thank You for creating me for relationship. Teach me to walk in wisdom when it comes to who I allow to influence my life. Help me to guard my heart, raise my standards, and align my connections with Your purpose. Surround me with people who love You and challenge me to grow. In Jesus' name. Amen.

28

Lay Aside Every Weight

"Therefore, since we are surrounded by such a great cloud of witnesses, let us throw off everything that hinders and the sin that so easily entangles. And let us run with perseverance the race marked out for us" (Hebrews 12:1).

You are in a race. Not a sprint, but a long-distance run, a race of faith, purpose, and perseverance. God has not only enrolled you in this race, but He has marked out a specific course for your life. You are not running aimlessly. Your race has direction, purpose, and eternal significance.

But if you're going to run well, you must travel light.

1. GOD HAS MAPPED OUT THE COURSE

You're not running in someone else's race. Your path is uniquely designed by God—custom-built for your calling, your gifts, and your assignment. But to finish well, you must be prepared for the journey.

You can't carry everything with you.

2. THIS RACE REQUIRES ENDURANCE

This is not about speed—it's about faithful endurance. You will face hills, opposition, and weariness. But God's grace is sufficient. Still, it will take spiritual discipline and focus to stay the course.

3. THE CROWD IS CHEERING YOU ON

You're not alone. Heaven is watching. The "great cloud of witnesses"—those who ran before you—are urging you to keep going. They are proof that it's possible to overcome, endure, and finish strong.

4. SHED EVERY WEIGHT

Not everything that weighs you down is sinful—but it can still slow you down.

Weights can be:
- Unnecessary commitments
- Fear of others' opinions
- Past hurts
- Distractions
- Emotional baggage

If it's hindering your walk with God or delaying your obedience, it's a weight that must be laid aside.

5. STRIP OFF THE SIN

Some things are not just heavy, they are dangerous.
Sin entangles. It binds. It trips you up and steals your focus.
You can't run freely while chained to compromise.

Repentance isn't about guilt, it's about freedom. Stripping away sin clears the way for you to run with joy, strength, and focus.

REFLECTION

1. What weights are you carrying that God never asked you to bear?
2. Is there a sin that's entangling your feet and slowing your progress?
3. What would it look like to lay it aside today?

PRAYER

Lord, I thank You for the race You've set before me. Help me to run with endurance, not distracted by the noise around me or the burdens I've carried for too long. Give me the courage to lay aside every weight, and the humility to repent of any sin that entangles me. I want to run free and finish strong, for Your glory. In Jesus' name. Amen.

29

Breaking Free from Deception

"Then you will know the truth, and the truth will set you free" (John 8:32).

Deception is subtle. It never announces itself boldly. It wears the mask of truth, wrapping falsehood in just enough familiarity to feel safe. But deception is bondage. It is one of Satan's most effective weapons, because it attacks the mind, distorts reality, and slowly detaches us from truth.

First Timothy 4:1 warns us clearly: "The Holy Spirit tells us clearly that in the last times some will turn away from the true faith; they will follow deceptive spirits and teachings that come from demons."

1. THE SOURCE OF DECEPTION

Satan's strategy is not always outright evil—it's manipulated truth. His goal?

- Influence
- Control
- Ownership

He deceives by planting lies, twisting Scripture, appealing to ego, and disguising error in "light."

Jesus said in John 8:44 that Satan is "a liar and the father of lies." His darts include:

- Lies that challenge God's identity or yours.
- Temptations that disguise bondage as freedom.
- Accusations that chain you in guilt and shame.

2. THE BONDAGE OF BELIEVING LIES

"People are in bondage to the lies they believe."
Every lie embraced as truth will shape your life as if it were true.

- A lie about your worth affects how you live.
- A lie about God's goodness limits your faith.
- A lie about sin blurs your convictions.

Deception alters your perception, and perception shapes your decisions.

3. SELF-DECEPTION IS THE MOST DANGEROUS KIND

The enemy doesn't have to lie to you if you're lying to yourself. Scripture warns against:

- Hearing God's Word but not doing it (James 1:22).
- Claiming to be without sin (1 John 1:8).
- Thinking you're spiritually mature while lacking self-control (James 1:26).
- Associating with ungodly influences thinking they won't affect you (1 Corinthians 15:33).

You cannot walk in freedom until you confront the lies you've accepted.

4. HOW TO BREAK FREE

- **Discern the lie.** Ask the Holy Spirit to reveal areas of deception.
- **Confront the lie.** You cannot change what you do not confront.
- **Replace the lie with truth.** God's Word is your weapon.
- **Live by the truth.** Power comes when you act on what you know.

5. DISCERNMENT IS KEY

Spiritual discernment is the ability to distinguish between truth and error.

John 2:24–25 shows us that Jesus knew what was in the hearts of people. Ask God for discernment—not just for others, but for yourself.

REFLECTION
1. Are there lies you've believed about yourself, God, or others?
2. Are you tolerating influences that are dulling your spiritual clarity?
3. Have you exchanged truth for something more comfortable but less biblical?

PRAYER

Lord, open my eyes to any deception that I've embraced. Expose every lie—whether from the enemy, others, or myself—and replace it with Your truth. Give me discernment to know what is of You and what is not. I choose truth over comfort, conviction over compromise, and freedom over bondage. In Jesus' name. Amen.

30

Freedom from the Voice of Accusation

"For the accuser of our brothers and sisters, who accuses them before our God day and night, has been hurled down" (Revelation 12:10).

There is an unseen battle that rages in the hearts and minds of believers—a battle not only against sin but against accusation. Satan is described as the "accuser of the brethren," and his attacks are relentless. Day and night, he seeks to remind you of every failure, every shortcoming, every reason why you don't deserve God's grace.

But here is the truth: his accusations are built on lies.

1. THE SOURCE OF ACCUSATION

John 8:44 tells us that Satan is "a liar and the father of lies." His accusations are not rooted in righteousness but in deception. His goal is to make you believe:

- You're too dirty to be clean.
- You're too broken to be healed.
- You've failed too much to be used by God.

But what he doesn't want you to remember is this: Jesus already dealt with your guilt.

2. JESUS, YOUR ADVOCATE

Zechariah 3 gives us a powerful picture: Satan accuses Joshua the high priest, pointing out his filthy garments. But God doesn't agree with Satan—He rebukes him and removes the filthy garments, replacing them with robes of righteousness.

This is your reality in Christ:

- Jesus is your defense attorney (1 John 2:1).
- God is the Judge who has already declared you righteous (2 Corinthians 5:21).
- You now wear garments of grace, not guilt.

3. CONVICTION VS. CONDEMNATION

The Holy Spirit brings conviction to lead you toward repentance and restoration.

Satan brings accusation to trap you in shame and despair.

Second Corinthians 7:10 says, "Godly sorrow brings repentance that leads to salvation . . . but worldly sorrow brings death."

If it leads you back to God, it's conviction.

If it pushes you away from God, it's accusation.

4. NO CONDEMNATION IN CHRIST

Romans 8:1 declares:

"There is therefore now no condemnation to them which are in Christ Jesus."

Let that settle your heart: You are not condemned. You are covered. Every time Satan points to your past, point to the cross.

REFLECTION

1. Are you carrying shame God has already forgiven?
2. Are you listening to the voice of the accuser more than the voice of your Advocate?
3. What would change if you truly believed you were clothed in righteousness?

PRAYER

Father, I thank You that I am no longer under condemnation. When the enemy accuses, remind me of the finished work of the cross. Help me to silence every lie with Your truth. Thank You for clothing me in righteousness, not because of what I've done, but because of what Jesus has done for me. I choose to walk in freedom, grace, and boldness. In Jesus' name. Amen.

31

"How Can This Be?"

"Then said Mary unto the angel, How shall this be, seeing I know not a man?" (Luke 1:34, KJV).

Have you ever stood at the crossroads of a promise and impossibility? Faced with a word from God that defies logic, reason, or natural process? Mary, a young virgin, did. When the angel Gabriel announced she would give birth to the Son of God, her response was honest and human: "How can this be?"

Maybe you're in a season where God has spoken something over your life that seems out of reach. He's called you to start a business, lead a ministry, heal a broken relationship, or believe for something miraculous—and you look at your resources, your history, your weaknesses, and ask the same question: "How can this be?"

God is not intimidated by your question. He didn't rebuke Mary for asking. Instead, He revealed the secret: "The Holy Ghost shall come upon thee, and the power of the Highest shall overshadow thee . . ." (Luke 1:35). The answer to your "how" is not found in your ability, but in God's power. What is impossible with man is always possible with God.

"How can this be?" moments are not signs of doubt; they're invitations to deeper faith. They're the pivot points where you stop depending on your understanding and start leaning on divine intervention.

Just like Mary, you may not understand the process, but you can still say, "Be it unto me according to thy word" (Luke 1:38). That surrender is the door through which the miraculous enters.

REFLECTION

1. Are you facing a "How can this be?" moment right now?

Surrender your logic, fears, and limitations to God. His Spirit is still overshadowing the impossible and birthing the extraordinary.

PRAYER

Lord, I bring You all my questions, especially the ones that begin with "How can this be?" Remind me that I don't need to have the answers—I only need to trust the One who does. Let Your power work in me and through me. Be it unto me according to Your Word. In Jesus' name. Amen.

32

Praying for Your Children

"Arise, cry out in the night: in the beginning of the watches pour out thine heart like water before the face of the LORD: lift up thy hands toward him for the life of thy young children . . ." (Lamentations 2:19, KJV).

As a parent, your most powerful role is not just provider or protector—it is intercessor. Prayer is your greatest privilege and most effective tool in shaping your child's life. It gives you access to God's throne on their behalf, even when they are out of your reach or understanding.

1. PRAYER IS YOUR GREATEST PRIVILEGE

God has given you the sacred responsibility of covering your children in prayer. Lamentations 2:19 paints a powerful image—parents pouring out their hearts like water before the Lord, pleading for the lives of their children. This is not a casual whisper—it's a cry of desperation, dependence, and deep love. Never underestimate the power of your voice in heaven on behalf of your children.

2. PRAY TO SHAPE DESTINY

"My voice shalt thou hear in the morning, O LORD; in the morning will I direct my prayer unto thee, and will look up" (Psalm 5:3, KJV).

Your prayers are not just reactions—they are tools of formation. Each prayer shapes destiny. Each word spoken in faith becomes part of the spiritual foundation upon which your child's future is built. You're not just asking for blessings—you're planting seeds of divine purpose.

3. RELEASE CONTROL TO GOD'S WILL

There comes a time when parenting means letting go and trusting God. True prayer isn't about controlling the outcome but surrendering it. It's saying, "Lord, I trust You more than I trust myself. Do in them what I cannot do." Praying for God's will is the highest form of love—it invites heaven's plan over your own.

4. YOUR PRAYERS ARE PROPHETIC

When you pray over your children, you're not predicting the future—you're writing it. You are declaring what God says about them, even if you don't yet see it. Speak life. Speak truth. Speak purpose. Don't just react to what is—proclaim what can be in Christ.

5. PRAY FOR GOD'S FAVOR

Favor is the fingerprint of God on your child's life. It's the open doors they couldn't open, the protection they don't even know they need, the blessings they didn't earn. Pray that God will surround them with favor like a shield (Psalm 5:12). Favor will take them where talent and effort alone never could.

REFLECTION

1. What are you believing for in your children's lives?
2. Have you surrendered your expectations and fears to God?

Begin today to speak prayers not just of protection, but of purpose, destiny, and favor.

PRAYER

Lord, thank You for the gift of my children. Today I lay them before You. I pour out my heart like water and ask You to shape their destiny, guard their steps, and fill their hearts with Your truth. I release my plans and embrace Yours. Let Your favor go before them. Write their story with Your grace. In Jesus' name. Amen.

33

The Habit of Prayer

"Pray without ceasing" (1 Thessalonians 5:17, KJV).

Prayer is not just discipline, it's a lifeline. But let's be honest: the idea of "praying without ceasing" can feel overwhelming. How can we possibly pray all the time?

1. PRAYER IS INTENTIONAL

The truth is, you won't pray anywhere and everywhere until you first start praying somewhere. Prayer begins with intentionality—a decision to carve out space in your life for God. That "somewhere" might be a quiet corner of your home, your car during your commute, or even just a few moments before your feet hit the floor in the morning. But it has to start somewhere.

2. PRAYER BECOMES A HABIT

From there, prayer becomes a habit—not a ritual, but a rhythm. A habit is something you do so regularly that it becomes second nature. And here's the powerful thing: habits don't just reflect who you are, they shape who you are. When prayer becomes a habit of the heart, it becomes the atmosphere of your life.

3. PRAYER KEEPS US GROUNDED

To pray without ceasing doesn't mean speaking words nonstop—it means living in continual awareness of God's presence, bringing every situation, decision, joy, or pain into conversation with Him. It's talking to God as often as you can, about everything you can—not just when things fall apart, but when they fall into place too.

But life has a way of pulling us in the opposite direction. Our situation stress, pressure, grief, or even success—can distract us or disconnect us. If we're not careful, we'll let life's noise drown out God's voice. But prayer reconnects us. It keeps us grounded, anchored, and aware of what matters most.

REFLECTION

1. Have you made prayer a habit—or just a reaction?
2. Where is your somewhere?

Start there and watch how prayer flows into every other part of your day.

PRAYER

Lord, teach me to pray without ceasing. Help me find a place to start and give me the grace to stay consistent. Let prayer become my habit, not just in crisis but in calm. May my heart stay tuned to Your voice throughout every moment of my day. In Jesus' name. Amen.

34

Living a Prayer-Filled, Purpose-Driven Life

"Devote yourselves to prayer, being watchful and thankful. And pray for us, too, that God may open a door for our message . . . Be wise in the way you act toward outsiders; make the most of every opportunity. Let your conversation be always full of grace, seasoned with salt . . ." (Colossians 4:2–6).

The apostle Paul gives us a powerful and practical blueprint for the believer's daily walk—one rooted in prayer, purpose, and people.

1. DEVOTION TO PRAYER WITH WATCHFULNESS AND GRATITUDE

Paul doesn't just tell us to pray—he tells us to devote ourselves to it. Prayer isn't a side dish to the Christian life; it is the main course. It's where we gain strength, receive direction, and remain spiritually alert. Like Peter's call to be sober and vigilant, prayer keeps our spiritual eyes open. It develops discernment and sensitivity to God's voice. And while we watch, we also give thanks—because gratitude keeps our hearts tender and expectant.

2. PRAY FOR THE FRONTLINES OF MINISTRY

Paul, even from prison, doesn't ask for comfort—he asks for clarity. He knew that the message of Christ needed bold, clear proclamation. Your prayers for pastors, missionaries, and leaders matter. You may not preach on stages, but you can partner in power through your prayers—asking God to open doors and give words that pierce hearts and reveal Christ.

3. WISE LIVING BEFORE THE WORLD

Your walk is a witness. The world is watching—not for perfection, but for authenticity. Wisdom in our behavior means choosing grace over grumbling, kindness over criticism, and faith over fear. Let your actions reflect the One you follow.

4. MAKE THE MOST OF EVERY OPPORTUNITY

Time is one of your most sacred resources. Every conversation, every encounter, every moment is a chance to reflect Jesus. Don't let moments slip by unused. Be intentional. Listen well. Serve others. Invest your time in things that matter for eternity.

5. QUALITY CONVERSATIONS THAT REFLECT CHRIST

Paul emphasizes not just what we say, but how we say it:
- **Full of grace.** Speak with kindness, understanding, and patience.
- **Seasoned with salt.** Add value. Bring flavor and truth into people's lives. Let your words uplift, not tear down.
- **Know how to answer everyone.** This requires wisdom, humility, and a heart anchored in God's Word.

REFLECTION

1. How devoted are you to prayer?
2. Are you using your time and words wisely?

Consider one way today you can grow in each of these five areas. Small steps can lead to big transformation.

PRAYER

Father, teach me to live a life of prayer—alert, thankful, and devoted. I lift up those preaching Your Word; give them clarity and boldness. Help me walk wisely, speak graciously, and use every opportunity for Your glory. Let my life reflect Christ—in both word and deed. In Jesus' name. Amen.

35

Blessed to Multiply

"Taking the five loaves and the two fish and looking up to heaven, He gave thanks and broke them. Then He gave them to the disciples to set before the people. They all ate and were satisfied, and the disciples picked up twelve basketfuls of broken pieces that were left over" (Luke 9:16–17).

Ministry often begins with a sense of lack. We look at the needs around us and then look at what we have in our hands—and it doesn't seem like enough. Whether it's our time, our resources, our gifts, or our energy, what we have may feel small in comparison to what is required. But this story reminds us that small in our hands becomes sufficient in God's hands.

When Jesus was faced with a hungry crowd, He didn't complain about the little. He didn't dismiss the offering as insufficient. Instead, He looked up, gave thanks, and blessed it. That moment of gratitude and blessing was the turning point. What seemed insignificant became abundant because He acknowledged the Source—His Father in heaven.

1. BLESS WHAT YOU HAVE

Before anything multiplied, Jesus gave thanks. Don't wait for the miracle to be grateful. Start with what's in your hand, and speak blessing over it. Thank God for the little, and watch how He begins to stretch it beyond what you imagined.

2. PARTNER WITH GOD THROUGH FAITH

Blessing and faith walk side by side. Faith sees potential where others see limitation. When you bless your time, your gifts, your finances, your ministry—no matter how small—you are declaring, "God, I trust You to do what only You can do."

3. MINISTRY FLOWS THROUGH OBEDIENT HANDS

Jesus gave the multiplied provision back to the disciples to distribute. The miracle didn't stop with the blessing—it continued through the obedience of the disciples. Ministry is often the miracle of simply showing up, taking what God has given, and placing it into the hands of others.

4. GOD'S ABUNDANCE ALWAYS LEAVES OVERFLOW

Everyone ate and was satisfied—and there were leftovers. When God blesses, He doesn't just meet the need; He exceeds it. The twelve baskets of broken pieces were a testimony that God is never limited. He is the God of more than enough.

REFLECTION

1. What do you have in your hands today that feels too small?
2. Have you taken time to bless it and thank God for it?

Offer it back to Him in faith—and trust that He will multiply it for His glory.

PRAYER

Lord, I thank You for what You've placed in my hands. Even when it feels small, I choose to bless it and trust You to multiply it. Use my life, my gifts, and my service to meet the needs of others. Let Your abundance flow through my faith and obedience. In Jesus' name. Amen.

36

The Blessing That Flows Through Generations

"Then Simeon blessed them and said . . ." (Luke 2:34).

In the quiet corners of the temple, as Mary and Joseph brought their infant Son to be dedicated, a faithful servant of God named Simeon stepped into a sacred moment. Holding Jesus in his arms, he blessed Him—and not only Him, but His parents as well. This was no ordinary moment. It was a divine declaration that the blessing of God is not just for the individual, but for the family, the future, and the world.

From His very birth, the life of Jesus was marked by blessing. And this scene reminds us that God's blessing is not reserved for the spectacular or the seasoned—it rests on the humble, the faithful, and even the newborn. Simeon's words echo the truth that God's love and favor are active from our very beginning.

1. GOD'S BLESSING BEGINS BEFORE WE UNDERSTAND IT

Before Jesus ever preached a sermon or performed a miracle, He was blessed. Before we speak, serve, or succeed, we too are recipients of God's love and intention. You are not working for God's blessing—you are working from it. His love is not earned; it is given.

2. BLESSING IS MEANT TO OVERFLOW TO FAMILIES

Simeon didn't just bless Jesus—he blessed Mary and Joseph as well. God's heart is for households, not just individuals. He desires for His love, peace, and favor to flow from person to person, generation to generation. Whether you're a parent, grandparent, sibling, or friend, your life can carry the blessing of God into the lives of those around you.

3. THE BLESSING COMES THROUGH THE SON AND BY THE SPIRIT

The love of the Father flows to us through Jesus, and that blessing is continually ministered to us by the Holy Spirit. It's not a one-time event—it's a daily reality. As believers, we walk in a living blessing that covers our past, empowers our present, and speaks hope into our future.

REFLECTION

1. Do you live with the awareness that you are blessed by God—before you perform, achieve, or prove yourself?
2. Have you spoken blessings over your family, your children, or your community lately?

PRAYER

Father, thank You that Your blessing rests on me—not because of what I've done, but because of who You are. Thank You for loving me from the very beginning and for allowing that love to flow through Jesus and into every area of my life. Help me carry that blessing to others and speak life, grace, and hope into the hearts of those around me. In Jesus' name. Amen.

37

Speak, Lord – I'm Listening

"The LORD came and stood there, calling as at the other times, 'Samuel! Samuel!' Then Samuel said, 'Speak, for your servant is listening'" (1 Samuel 3:10).

Too often, we come to God bursting with our own ideas, complaints, and agendas. But the posture of true discipleship is not speaking first; it's listening. Like young Samuel, we must learn to quiet our hearts before the Lord and say, "Speak, for Your servant is listening."

Listening is not passive; it is active surrender. It is a declaration that God's voice matters more than our thoughts, and His direction is more valuable than our plans.

1. WE NEED GOD'S LOVE COMMUNICATED DAILY

"Let the morning bring me word of your unfailing love, for I have put my trust in you" (Psalm 143:8).

Each day begins best when we hear from God. His love is not just a concept—it's a voice we need to hear regularly.

- His love brings confidence when we feel uncertain.
- It is unfailing, never running out or running dry.
- It brings peace in chaos.
- It gives assurance when doubts try to dominate.

2. THE IMPORTANCE OF KNOWING HIS WAYS EVERY MORNING

We weren't designed to figure life out on our own. We need fresh direction daily. That's why David prayed, "Show me the way I should go, for to you I entrust my life" (Psalm 143:8).

Just as the Israelites depended on daily manna, we depend on God's guidance. Yesterday's word was good—but today needs a new one. Morning by morning, He desires to lead us.

3. ENTRUSTING YOUR LIFE FULLY TO GOD

When we know His voice—"My sheep listen to My voice; I know them, and they follow Me" (John 10:27)—we stop inviting God into our agenda. Instead, we surrender our entire life to His. We don't ask God to bless our plans; we ask Him to reveal His. That shift changes everything.

REFLECTION

1. Are you listening for God's voice each morning? Or are you still trying to lead on your own? Start your day not with noise, but with surrender.

Ask God to speak and be willing to follow.

PRAYER

Lord, teach me to listen before I speak. Let my mornings be marked by the sound of Your unfailing love. Lead me in the way I should go. I entrust my life—not just my plans—to You. Speak, Lord. Your servant is listening. In Jesus' name. Amen.

38

Living Ready, Serving Well

"The end of all things is near. Therefore, be alert and of sober mind so that you may pray . . . Above all, love each other deeply . . . Each of you should use whatever gift you have received to serve others, as faithful stewards of God's grace . . ." (1 Peter 4:7–11).

The apostle Peter calls believers to live with urgency, purpose, and love. His words are both a wake-up call and a guide for how to live meaningfully in challenging times. When the world feels uncertain and chaotic, the believer is not called to panic, but to pray, love, and serve. This is a lifestyle of alertness, not anxiety.

1. UNDERSTAND THE TIMES

Peter begins with a sobering reminder: "The end of all things is near." This isn't meant to instill fear, but clarity.

- Like the sons of Issachar, who "understood the times and knew what Israel should do" (1 Chronicles 12:32), we must pray for discernment.
- Knowing the times and seasons of our lives helps us move in step with God—not ahead of Him, and not behind.
- Without that discernment, disappointment can settle in when our expectations don't align with God's timing.

2. BE ALERT AND SOBER

Peter urges us to be clear-minded so that we can pray effectively. A sober mind is one that isn't clouded by fear, distraction, or emotional extremes.

- Be mindful of your walk—how you live.
- Be mindful of your talk—what you say.
- Even your body language communicates your readiness and faith.

3. BE A PERSON OF PRAYER

Prayer is not just a reaction—it's preparation. It's where we align our hearts with God's will and intercede for a world in need. In the last days, it is not charisma or cleverness that will sustain you—it is communion with God.

4. LOVE DEEPLY

"Above all, love each other deeply, because love covers a multitude of sins" (1 Peter 4:8).

Deep love is not surface-level kindness. It's commitment. It's forgiveness. It's grace upon grace. In a world growing cold, let your love burn bright.

5. PRACTICE HOSPITALITY

Open your home, your heart, and your life to others. And do it without grumbling. Hospitality is an extension of love. It says, "You're welcome here—just as you are."

6. SERVE WITHOUT COMPLAINING

Grumbling weakens the beauty of serving. Whatever you do—whether it's behind the scenes or on the front lines—do it with joy. God values how you serve just as much as what you do.

7. USE YOUR GIFTS TO SERVE OTHERS

You have been gifted by God, not for self-promotion, but for service. Whether speaking, teaching, helping, or encouraging—do it with excellence and humility. Your gifts are tools to reflect God's grace.

8. BE A FAITHFUL STEWARD OF GRACE

God's grace is multifaceted. It shows up in different forms through different people. Stewarding it means using what God has given you wisely, generously, and consistently—always pointing back to Him.

REFLECTION
1. Are you living with purpose in light of eternity?
2. What season are you in—and how are you stewarding God's grace in that season?

PRAYER

Lord, help me to understand the times and walk in step with Your Spirit. Keep me alert, sober, and prayerful. Teach me to love deeply, serve humbly, and use my gifts faithfully. May my life bring glory to You in all things. In Jesus' name. Amen.

39

The Power of Remaining

"If you remain in me and my words remain in you, ask whatever you wish, and it will be done for you" (John 15:7).

At the heart of every fruitful Christian life is one word: remain. Jesus invites us into a relationship that is not rushed or superficial, but deep, enduring, and rooted in Him. The promise in this verse is powerful—answered prayer—but the condition is clear: remaining.

1. UNION WITH CHRIST

Remaining begins with relationships. Before we ever chose Him, He chose us. Like a branch joined to the vine, we are united to Christ through the Gardener—God the Father—who by His mercy grafts us into Jesus. This union is not based on performance but on grace. Remaining means drawing life from Him, continually connected in spirit, depending on His strength.

2. OBEDIENCE TO THE WORD

Jesus says His words must remain in us. That means obedience—not out of duty, but out of love. As His Word shapes our thinking and our hearts, it aligns our desires with His will. Our prayers then reflect His purpose, and we begin to see them answered not because we've demanded something, but because we've desired rightly. Obedience is the fruit of true connection.

3. REST IN HIS LOVE

Remaining also means resting. In a world of striving and stress, Jesus offers rest—not just from burdens but in His love. You don't have to earn His affection. You don't have to prove yourself to stay connected. You remain by trusting. His love is constant, and your place in Him is secure. Peace comes when we stop trying to hold on and instead abide in the One who is holding us.

REFLECTION
1. Are you rushing through your days, or are you remaining in Christ?
2. Is your prayer life shaped more by panic or by peace?

True fruitfulness flows from connection—not effort.

PRAYER

Jesus, teach me to remain. Help me to stay rooted in You—resting in Your love, obeying Your Word, and trusting in our union. Let my prayers rise from a place of connection, not desperation. May I live a life that bears fruit because I'm found in You. In Your name. Amen.

40

A Blessed Nation Begins with a Praying Church

"Blessed is the nation whose God is the LORD, the people he chose for his inheritance" (Psalm 33:12).

We often long for national blessings. We desire peace, justice, prosperity, and righteousness to flow through the land. But too often, we look to politicians or policies to make it happen. And when they fail—we inevitably lose hope in the system. But Scripture reminds us that the true transformation of a nation does not begin in the palace or the parliament but begins in the prayer closet.

God declares a nation blessed when He is Lord—not merely in word or tradition, but in the hearts of its people. This kind of national blessing isn't the product of legislation, but of salvation. And the Church has a vital role in bringing it to pass.

Paul writes in 1 Timothy 2:1–4 that believers are to engage in petitions, prayers, intercession, and thanksgiving—for all people, and especially for kings and those in authority. Why? Because our prayers do more than preserve personal peace—they help shape the spiritual atmosphere of a nation.

1. PRAY FOR ALL PEOPLE

Every soul matters to God. Our prayers should be inclusive and compassionate. Whether near or far, like us or different, every person is someone Christ died for. When we pray for others, we align ourselves with God's heart for the world.

2. PRAY FOR LEADERS AND AUTHORITIES

Praying for those in power is not about political alignment, it's about spiritual responsibility. Leadership influences culture, policy, and national values. When we intercede for those in authority, we create the spiritual conditions for godliness to rise and corruption to fall.

3. THE FRUIT: GODLINESS, HOLINESS, AND PEACE

Paul connects this kind of intercessory prayer to a transformed society—one marked by godliness, holiness, and peace. This isn't passive peace; it's a peace birthed through spiritual warfare and persistent prayer. It's the kind of peace that fosters safety, dignity, and moral clarity.

4. IT PLEASES GOD AND OPENS HEARTS

Ultimately, this kind of praying pleases God. Why? Because it opens the door for what He desires most—salvation. When we pray for our nation, we're not just asking for political solutions—we're partnering with heaven to bring eternal change. The salvation of souls is God's ultimate goal, and it is what truly makes a nation blessed.

REFLECTION

1. Are your prayers shaping your nation?
2. Are you engaging your spiritual responsibility as part of Christ's Church to pray for people and leaders?

PRAYER

Father, thank You for the blessing promised to the nation that calls You Lord. Forgive us for relying too much on systems and too little on Your Spirit. Teach us to pray with faith and fervency—for all people, and for our leaders. Let our intercession open the door for salvation, godliness, and peace in our land. May our prayers create an atmosphere where You are truly Lord. In Jesus' name. Amen.

41

Walking on Level Ground

"Teach me to do your will, for you are my God; may your good Spirit lead me on level ground" (Psalm 143:10).

To walk on level ground is not to walk in a life free of hardship. It doesn't mean there won't be valleys, steep climbs, or rough terrain. In fact, Scripture is clear that we will face trials of many kinds. But the "level ground" David speaks of is not circumstantial—it's spiritual. It refers to the steadiness of soul and maturity of character that comes from walking closely with God and being led by His Spirit.

Level ground is how you respond to life, not how life responds to you.

1. LEVEL GROUND IS SPIRITUAL MATURITY

It's a life that remains steady when the world shakes. It's the stability that comes when your mind is renewed and your will is surrendered to God's. You are not driven by emotion or reaction, but by purpose and the Spirit. You walk in wisdom, in discernment, and in peace.

Isaiah 26:7 affirms this: "The path of the righteous is level; you, the Upright One, make the way of the righteous smooth." This doesn't mean ease—it means alignment with God's direction. Righteousness brings clarity, and clarity brings stability.

2. LEVEL GROUND LEADERS KNOW THE ENEMY

To walk in the Spirit is to be spiritually aware. You are not ignorant of the enemy's schemes (2 Corinthians 2:11). But you don't fight from fear—you fight from focus. Just like the Secret Service learns to spot a counterfeit by studying the real thing, a believer grows in discernment not by obsessing over darkness, but by becoming deeply familiar with the light.

When your mind is conformed to God's will, you instinctively recognize what is not from Him. Jesus, walking in perfect discernment, identified Satan's influence behind Peter's words (Matthew 16:23). That's level-ground leadership—seeing the true source behind the surface.

3. LEVEL GROUND RESPONDS, NOT REACTS

When Nehemiah faced threats meant to discourage and stop the work of rebuilding, he didn't react in fear. He prayed: "Now strengthen my hands" (Nehemiah 6:9).

A mature believer doesn't just identify the enemy's strategy—they know how to respond. Not with panic, but with prayer. Not with anger, but with strength. Not with retreat, but with resolve.

Job's wife faltered in the fire, but Job, though shaken, held to his faith. Level ground doesn't mean perfect composure—but it does mean your foundation holds, even when your world doesn't.

REFLECTION

1. Are you walking on level ground today?
2. Is your mind conformed to God's will, or are you swayed by the highs and lows of life?

Let the Spirit of God lead you into steady, strong maturity—so you can respond to life with wisdom, faith, and strength.

PRAYER

Father, teach me to do Your will. Lead me by Your Spirit onto level ground—not so that life will be easy, but so that I will be steady. Make me discerning, grounded, and Spirit-led. Help me to know the enemy's tactics and to respond with faith, not fear. Strengthen my hands, Lord, and make my steps sure. In Jesus' name. Amen.

42

Eyes That See More

"For this reason, ever since I heard about your faith in the Lord Jesus and your love for all God's people, I have not stopped giving thanks for you, remembering you in my prayers" (Ephesians 1:15–16).

Paul was writing to believers who were already walking in faith and love. Yet his prayer wasn't simply for their blessings to increase or for their circumstances to improve; it was for their understanding to deepen. He longed for them to know Christ more intimately and fully. This tells us something crucial: there are always deeper levels in knowing God.

1. SPIRIT OF WISDOM AND REVELATION

Paul prayed that the Ephesian believers would receive a spirit of wisdom and revelation so that they could know Jesus better. Not just know *about* Him—but know *Him*. That means even the most mature believer still has room to grow. Revelation isn't just knowledge. It's insight, divine perspective, and spiritual clarity that open the eyes of our understanding.

Knowing God better is not automatic. It comes by the Spirit, and it requires humility, hunger, and a willingness to keep learning.

2. EYES OF THE HEART ENLIGHTENED

Paul speaks of the eyes of your heart—a powerful metaphor. The heart is the center of belief, desire, and devotion. But before the heart can see, it must be enlightened. The Spirit must illuminate what is often hidden beneath the surface of our natural thinking.

What happens when our hearts are enlightened?

a. We See the Hope to Which He Has Called Us

This isn't just wishful thinking—it's a confident expectation anchored in God's promises. When you know Christ deeply, you don't just endure life—you walk in divine purpose, knowing that your calling is sacred and secure.

b. We See the Riches of His Glorious Inheritance in His Holy People

God sees His people as treasure, and He places His riches among them. When we walk in revelation, we begin to value the Church—not as an organization, but as a community filled with God's presence, gifting, and grace.

c. We See His Incomparably Great Power for Us Who Believe

This is not distant power for us. It's resurrection power, working within and through us. But we only walk in that power to the degree we see it, believe it, and respond to it.

REFLECTION

1. Are you content with what you know of Christ, or are you hungry to know Him more?
2. Are the eyes of your heart clear and open, or clouded by distraction, fear, or complacency?

Ask the Lord today for the spirit of wisdom and revelation—He delights to give it.

PRAYER

Lord, thank You for the faith You've given me and for the community of believers around me. I ask today for the spirit of wisdom and revelation so I may know You better. Enlighten the eyes of my heart to see the hope of my calling, the riches among Your people, and the power You've made available to me through Christ. Open my heart to know You more deeply each day. In Jesus' name. Amen.

43

The Gift of Perfect Peace

"Peace I leave with you, my peace I give unto you: not as the world giveth, give I unto you. Let not your heart be troubled, neither let it be afraid" (John 14:27, KJV).

In a world filled with chaos, conflict, and constant change, Jesus offers us a gift the world cannot give—peace. Not temporary relief or fleeting calm, but a deep, abiding, unshakable peace. It's His peace—born not from outward circumstances, but from inward confidence in the Father.

This peace is not the absence of trouble, but the presence of Christ. It's what steadies your soul when storms rage, when answers are delayed, and when the future feels uncertain. Jesus didn't say we won't have trouble—He said our hearts don't have to be troubled.

1. A PEACE THAT SURPASSES UNDERSTANDING

"And the peace of God, which passeth all understanding, shall keep your hearts and minds through Christ Jesus" (Philippians 4:7, KJV).

God's peace doesn't always make sense—it surpasses logic. You might be in the middle of grief, transition, or a spiritual battle, and yet feel anchored, calm, even joyful. That's not human peace—that's God's peace. It guards your heart from fear and your mind from spiraling thoughts. It's a protective force that keeps you grounded in Jesus, no matter what surrounds you.

2. PERFECT PEACE COMES FROM A STAYED MIND

"Thou wilt keep him in perfect peace, whose mind is stayed on thee: because he trusteth in thee" (Isaiah 26:3, KJV).

The key to sustained peace is focus. A stayed mind is a mind fixed on God—His Word, His promises, His character. When your thoughts wander to fear, anxiety, or control, peace leaks away. But when your mind is rooted in trust, you'll find a peace that perfectly holds you together in every season.

3. LET NOT YOUR HEART BE TROUBLED

Jesus gives us both a promise and a command: "Let not your heart be troubled." That means you have a choice. You can either surrender to fear or stand in faith. You can either absorb the panic of the world or receive the peace of Christ. His peace is a gift—ours to receive, but also ours to protect.

REFLECTION

1. Where is your mind fixed today?
2. What has been troubling your heart?

Jesus offers you His peace—a peace stronger than fear, deeper than pain, and greater than anything the world can offer.

PRAYER

Lord Jesus, thank You for the gift of peace—Your peace. Help me to fix my mind on You, to trust You completely, and to refuse fear. Let Your peace guard my heart and mind. Teach me to live anchored in You, no matter the circumstances. In Your name. Amen.

44

The God of All Comfort

"Praise be to the God and Father of our Lord Jesus Christ, the Father of compassion and the God of all comfort, who comforts us in all our troubles, so that we can comfort those in any trouble with the comfort we ourselves receive from God" (2 Corinthians 1:3–4).

In a world filled with pain, brokenness, and unanswered questions, we all long for comfort—not the kind that only soothes for a moment, but the kind that restores strength, brings hope, and lifts the heart. The apostle Paul introduces us to the One who offers exactly that: the God of all comfort and the Father of compassion.

1. THE FATHER OF COMPASSION

God is not distant from our suffering—He is moved by it. Compassion is deeper than sympathy or empathy. It's not just feeling for someone; it's acting on their behalf. Compassion sees pain, enters into it, and brings help. That is who God is.

- He doesn't look away from your struggle—He draws near.
- He doesn't just feel your sorrow—He moves to meet your need.

Compassion is God's nature. He treats our suffering not with indifference, but with tender mercy.

2. THE GOD OF ALL COMFORT

God's comfort is not the absence of pain, but the presence of peace in the midst of it. The word "comfort" here means to strengthen, to encourage, and to restore hope.

- God doesn't always remove the storm, but He anchors us in it.
- He gives us what we need to endure: grace, courage, and even joy.
- He turns grief into growth, and sorrow into testimony.

3. HE COMFORTS US IN ALL TROUBLES

There is no limit to the kind of trouble God meets us in. Whether it's physical pain, emotional distress, relational heartbreak, or spiritual doubt—He is present and faithful.

God doesn't promise a life free from trouble, but He promises we will never go through it alone. His comfort is not shallow; it is personal, deep, and sustaining.

4. COMFORTED TO COMFORT OTHERS

Here lies a divine purpose in our pain: that we may become instruments of comfort to others.

- Your story of how God met you becomes a source of strength for someone else.
- The comfort you receive becomes a gift you give.
- God builds a cycle of healing: the comforted become comforters.

This means we need both God's comfort and the community of the comforted. Your life, your testimony, your survival is someone else's hope.

REFLECTION

1. Have you received God's comfort in a difficult season?
2. Are you allowing your healing to become someone else's help?

Remember, your comfort isn't meant to end with you—it's meant to flow through you.

PRAYER

Father of compassion, thank You that You are close to the brokenhearted and faithful in every trial. Thank You for comforting me—not only to heal me, but to equip me to comfort others. Help me to be aware of those around me who need the same grace I've received. Let Your compassion flow through my life. In Jesus' name. Amen.

45

A Life That Commands Respect

"Command and teach these things. Don't let anyone look down on you because you are young, but set an example for the believers in speech, in conduct, in love, in faith and in purity . . . Be diligent in these matters; give yourself wholly to them, so that everyone may see your progress" (1 Timothy 4:11–15).

Ministry is not about age, title, or personality, it's about faithfulness. Paul's charge to Timothy was not to demand respect, but to live in a way that earns it. He didn't tell Timothy to argue his way into credibility, but to lead by example—through character, conduct, and consistent growth.

In a time when credibility in leadership is often questioned, God is still raising up people who lead not by dominance, but by integrity and devotion.

1. FOCUS ON WHAT YOU CAN CONTROL

There are aspects of ministry and leadership that are beyond your control, how people perceive you, how they respond to your call. But Paul reminds Timothy (and us) to steward what we do control:

- **Integrity:** Be the same person in private as you are in public. Let your word mean something.
- **Slothfulness:** Don't be lazy with your call. Ministry requires diligence and discipline.
- **Manipulation:** Avoid using your influence to control others. True leadership is servant-hearted.
- **Disloyalty:** Be faithful to your leaders, your calling, and the truth.

- **Misuse of Power:** Never leverage your position for personal advantage. The goal is service, not status.

These qualities reflect a heart anchored in Christ and earn the respect of others—not instantly, but inevitably.

2. WHEN YOU CAN'T CONTROL PERCEPTION

Sometimes, people will question your personhood, your proclamation, or your proficiency. You may feel dismissed because of your youth, your background, or your experience. When that happens, remember Paul's wisdom:

- Let your speech be gracious and truthful.
- Let your conduct be upright and consistent.
- Let your love be genuine and sacrificial.
- Let your faith be strong and unshakable.
- Let your purity be uncompromised and visible.

Over time, a faithful life speaks louder than any doubt or criticism.

3. LET THERE BE PROGRESS

Paul says, "Give yourself wholly to them, so that everyone may see your progress."

God doesn't expect perfection—but He does expect progress. Let your growth be evident:

- Grow in your knowledge of the Word.
- Grow in your ability to teach and lead.
- Grow in your prayer life and spiritual maturity.

Let those around you witness a life that is not static, but steadily becoming more like Christ.

4. WATCH CLOSELY – PERSEVERE FAITHFULLY

"Watch your life and doctrine closely." Why? Because you're not just living for yourself—you're leading others. Your faithfulness has eternal implications. Your perseverance can lead to salvation—not only for you, but for those who follow you.

REFLECTION
1. Are you diligently stewarding what you can control in your walk and ministry?
2. Are others able to see your progress?

PRAYER

Lord, help me to live in a way that honors You and earns the respect of others—not by title, but by character. Keep me diligent, faithful, and full of love. When I am overlooked or misunderstood, remind me that You see my heart. Help me to grow in wisdom, grace, and power as I lead. In Jesus' name. Amen.

46

Devoted to Prayer, Driven by Purpose

"Devote yourselves to prayer, being watchful and thankful. And pray for us, too, that God may open a door for our message, so that we may proclaim the mystery of Christ . . . Pray that I may proclaim it clearly, as I should. Be wise in the way you act toward outsiders . . . Let your conversation be always full of grace, seasoned with salt . . ." (Colossians 4:2–6).

The Christian life is not just about believing—it's about engaging. In his closing words to the church at Colossae, Paul gives a powerful framework for a life that impacts others through prayer, witness, wisdom, and grace.

1. THE IMPERATIVE OF PRAYER

Paul doesn't say, "If you have time, pray." He says, "Devote yourselves to prayer."

Prayer is not optional for a fruitful Christian life—it is essential. It's how we align with God's heart, receive wisdom, and intercede for others. Without prayer, our efforts are powerless; with it, even the impossible becomes possible.

a. **Developing a Personal Devotion**

A devoted prayer life is not built in a day—it is built by daily choice. Devotion means priority. It means showing up, whether you feel inspired or not. It's where intimacy with God grows, and faith is strengthened.

b. **Praying for Those Who Share the Gospel**

Paul, a bold apostle, asks for prayer. Why? Because even the most anointed need support. We must lift up pastors, evangelists, missionaries, and everyday believers sharing Christ. Their effectiveness is multiplied by our prayers.

c. Pray for Clarity in the Gospel Message

It's not enough to share—we must share clearly. The Gospel is simple, yet profound. Pray that those who preach would do so with clarity, courage, and compassion, so hearts are truly reached and transformed.

2. WISE INTERACTIONS WITH OUTSIDERS

"Be wise in the way you act toward outsiders; make the most of every opportunity" (Colossians 4:5).

The world is watching. Our lives often speak before our words. Wisdom in our actions builds bridges; foolishness burns them. Every moment, every relationship, is a chance to reveal Jesus. Don't wait for the perfect platform—your daily life is your mission field.

3. GRACE-FILLED CONVERSATIONS

"Let your conversation be always full of grace, seasoned with salt . . ." (Colossians 4:6).

Words have power. Grace-filled speech heals, uplifts, and reveals Christ. "Salted" words preserve truth and bring flavor—meaning, they make the Gospel attractive, not bland or bitter. We don't speak to win arguments—we speak to win hearts.

REFLECTION

1. Are you devoted to prayer?
2. Are your words and actions drawing people toward Christ or pushing them away?

Ask God to help you live, speak, and love in a way that opens doors for His message.

PRAYER

Lord, help me to live a life devoted to prayer. Let my heart be watchful and thankful. I lift up those who proclaim Your Gospel—grant them open doors and clear words. Teach me to walk wisely, to use every opportunity to reveal Your love, and to speak with grace and truth. May my life be a witness that leads others to You. In Jesus' name. Amen.

47

Priorities in Ministry

"Very early in the morning, while it was still dark, Jesus got up, left the house and went off to a solitary place, where he prayed . . . Jesus replied, 'Let us go somewhere else—to the nearby villages—so I can preach there also. That is why I have come'" (Mark 1:35, 38).

In Mark 1:32–38, we see a remarkable glimpse into the life and rhythm of Jesus' ministry. The crowds were gathering, miracles were happening, and needs were everywhere. Yet, right in the middle of great momentum and urgent demand, Jesus stepped away.

This passage teaches us a vital truth: Ministry is not just about doing the work—it's about doing the right work, the right way, with the right heart.

1. THE PRESSURE OF THE CROWDS

"That evening after sunset the people brought to Jesus all the sick and demon-possessed. The whole town gathered at the door" (Mark 1:32–33).

Jesus was surrounded by great need. The demands were real, and the expectations were high. The pressure to perform and continue healing was intense. Ministry—whether public or private—can be overwhelming when the needs of people seem endless. But Jesus shows us that being needed doesn't always mean being called in that moment.

2. LEAVING NEEDS UNMET

In a surprising move, Jesus walked away from the crowds the next morning. Not because He didn't care, but because He was obedient.

He left behind miracles He could have performed and people He could have helped—because He was following a greater priority: the will of the Father.

This is a difficult but freeing truth: You will never meet every need. And you're not meant to.

3. THE IMPORTANCE OF REST AND REPLENISHMENT

Jesus got up early and went to a solitary place to pray.

Ministry drained Him—not just physically, but emotionally and spiritually. If Jesus needed time to rest, replenish, and reconnect with the Father, how much more do we?

Burnout happens when we give out more than we take in. We must prioritize moments of stillness to refill what ministry pours out.

4. CLARITY FROM THE FATHER

In solitude, Jesus received fresh perspective. When the disciples came looking for Him, expecting Him to return to the crowd, He declared: "Let us go somewhere else . . . that is why I have come."

Jesus didn't allow the urgency of people to override the clarity of His purpose. His priorities were not shaped by popularity, but by intimacy with the Father.

REFLECTION

1. Are you allowing the noise of ministry—or life—to drown out the voice of God?
2. Are you driven by the demands of others, or are you being led by the Spirit?

Step away when needed. Rest. Pray. Refocus. Then move forward with divine clarity.

PRAYER

Lord, thank You for the example of Jesus, who shows us how to serve with wisdom and rest with purpose. Teach me to prioritize Your presence over people's pressure, and to pursue Your will above every demand. Help me to know when to pause, when to say no, and when to move forward with clarity. In Jesus' name. Amen.

48

Let Your Light Shine

"You are the light of the world. A town built on a hill cannot be hidden. Neither do people light a lamp and put it under a bowl. Instead they put it on its stand, and it gives light to everyone in the house. In the same way, let your light shine before others, that they may see your good deeds and glorify your Father in heaven" (Matthew 5:14–16).

Jesus did not say try to *be* the light—He said you *are* the light of the world. It's not a suggestion; it's a declaration of identity. The moment Christ lives in you, His light lives in you—and you are meant to shine.

1. LIGHT PRESUPPOSES DARKNESS

Light has meaning only in contrast to darkness. Jesus' words imply that the world is in spiritual darkness: confusion, sin, despair, and brokenness. And in the midst of that, God sends you as a light-bearer. Your presence, your attitude, your actions should push back the darkness.

2. WHAT HAPPENS IN DARKNESS?

In darkness, people stumble, get lost, and live in fear. Darkness represents deception, hopelessness, and separation from God. The world doesn't just need light—it's desperate for it. And God's plan to reach the world isn't just a sermon—it's you.

3. HOW DO WE OVERCOME DARKNESS?

The answer isn't to fight darkness with more darkness, but to shine. Light always wins. You don't have to strive—you simply have to shine. Darkness cannot withstand the presence of true light.

4. YOU ARE THE LIGHT

Not *will* be, not *might* be—you *are*. This is your identity in Christ. You carry His light in your words, your integrity, your kindness, your courage, and your compassion. Wherever you go, you carry the answer to the darkness around you.

5. OUR PURPOSE IS TO SHINE FOR OTHERS

Light is not for hiding—it's for revealing. Jesus said no one lights a lamp and hides it under a bowl. Our faith is meant to be public, visible, and impactful. Your life is a testimony, whether you speak or stay silent. Shine so others can see the way to the Father.

6. LIGHT = GOOD WORKS

Jesus defines light as good deeds. It's not just about what we believe, but how we live. When we love the unlovable, serve without expecting return, and show grace under pressure, we are shining light that others can't ignore.

7. PURPOSE OF THE LIGHT: GLORY TO THE FATHER

The goal of our shining is not attention, applause, or influence—it is worship. When people see your light, they are drawn not to you but to God. Your life becomes a signpost pointing to the Savior.

8. WHAT BOWLS ARE COVERING YOUR LIGHT?

Jesus warned that we can hide our light. What are the bowls we place over it?

- Fear – afraid of what others might think.
- Inconsistency – living one way on Sunday and another the rest of the week.
- Prejudice – choosing who we love based on preference, not Christ.
- Double-mindedness – wavering between the world and God.

It's time to uncover the light. The world is waiting.

REFLECTION

1. What kind of light are you shining today?
2. Is it hidden under fear or glowing with purpose?

Ask the Lord to remove any "bowl" that's covering your light so you can reflect His glory clearly.

PRAYER

Father, thank You for calling me the light of the world. Help me not to hide what You've placed in me. Strip away fear, compromise, and anything that dims Your light in my life. Let my good works reflect Your goodness, and may others glorify You through what they see in me. In Jesus' name. Amen.

49

Living for His Glory

"He has rescued us from the domain of darkness and transferred us to the kingdom of His beloved Son" (Colossians 1:13, NASB1995).

"Whether, then, you eat or drink or whatever you do, do all to the glory of God" (1 Corinthians 10:31, NASB1995).

"I glorified You on the earth, having accomplished the work which You have given Me to do" (John 17:4, NASB1995).

As a child of the King, your life is no longer random, aimless, or without meaning. You have been rescued—pulled from the shadows of confusion and futility and transferred into a new realm: the Kingdom of God's beloved Son. This isn't just a shift in location, it's a transformation of identity, purpose, and destiny.

1. YOU CANNOT HAVE GOD AND CHANCE

There is no such thing as coincidence in the Kingdom. A believer's life is not ruled by chance or fate, it is governed by divine design. You were created with intention, rescued with purpose, and positioned for impact. To live for God's glory means acknowledging that every moment, every decision, and every breath has weight in eternity.

2. IDENTITY SHAPES DESTINY

If you don't know who you are, you won't know where you're going. And even if you arrive, you won't recognize that you've made it. When you search for your identity apart from Christ, you wander in uncertainty. But when you embrace your identity as a new creation—redeemed, loved, empowered—you begin to function the way you were created to.

Misdefined identity leads to misdirected purpose.

Right identity unlocks divine destiny.

3. WHAT ARE GOOD WORKS?

Good works aren't random acts of kindness or self-made achievements. Biblically, good works are Spirit-led actions that:

- Benefit others in time and eternity
- Point people back to God
- Reflect the heart of the Father

When you walk in the good works God prepared for you (Ephesians 2:10), you manifest His presence. You become a living witness that God's Kingdom is active and alive in the world.

4. GLORY COMES THROUGH PURPOSE FULFILLED

Jesus glorified the Father not just by being good—but by finishing the work He was sent to do. He lived with focused obedience and completed His assignment. You glorify God in the same way:

- When you know your God-given identity.
- When you live with purpose.
- When your life becomes a testimony of God's wisdom, grace, and truth.

You were not created to coast—you were created to contribute. To impact others. To make Him known. You bring glory to God when you intentionally walk in your calling and finish the work He gave you to do.

REFLECTION

1. Are you living by chance or by calling?
2. Are you pursuing the works God has prepared for you, or are you still searching for who you are?

Ask the Lord to show you your identity in Him and clarify your path.

PRAYER

Father, thank You for rescuing me from darkness and transferring me into the Kingdom of Your Son. Help me to live with intentionality, not chance. Remind me daily of who I am in Christ, and lead me into the good works You have prepared for me. May my life bring You glory as I walk in obedience and purpose. In Jesus' name. Amen.

50

Kingdom-Minded Leadership

"The kingdom of God is not coming with signs to be observed . . . for behold, the kingdom of God is in your midst" (Luke 17:20–21, ESV).

"To them God has chosen to make known . . . the glorious riches of this mystery, which is Christ in you, the hope of glory" (Colossians 1:27).

What is the Kingdom of God? It is the presence and rule of the King—Jesus Christ—in and through our lives. It's not just a future destination; it's a present reality. The Kingdom is not merely about heaven one day—it's about heaven touching earth today through obedient, Christ-like people.

1. THE KINGDOM IS WITHIN AND AMONG US

Jesus told the Pharisees that the Kingdom is not a matter of outward observation but an inner reality: "The Kingdom is within you." When Christ dwells in us, the King has come to take His throne—and where the King rules, His Kingdom manifests. This includes both individual transformation and corporate expression through the Church.

The Kingdom of God is not just a private experience—it's a public movement expressed through His body.

2. FROM THE INDIVIDUAL JESUS TO THE CORPORATE CHRIST

Jesus is the Head—but now He has a body, the Church. Through the Church, Christ continues His work on earth. The presence of the Kingdom increases wherever Christ rules through His people.

This is why you cannot separate the Church from the Kingdom. The Church is the expression of the Kingdom, and through it, transformation comes to families, communities, and nations.

3. TRANSFORMATION IS THE EVIDENCE OF THE KINGDOM

Wherever the Kingdom is active, things change. Lives are healed. The broken are restored. Justice is pursued. Light overcomes darkness. A Kingdom-minded leader doesn't just lead programs, they pursue transformation. They measure fruit not by numbers alone, but by the visible reign of Christ.

4. THE CHARACTER OF A KINGDOM-MINDED LEADER

To be Kingdom-minded is to be Christ-like—and this happens through obedience.

- Obey the words of Jesus – His commands shape our conduct and mindset.
- Do the works of Jesus – What is He doing now? He is building His Church (Matthew 16:18).

We are living stones in that building (1 Peter 2:5). As leaders and believers, we are called to gather more "stones" (souls), and fit them into the house of God. But this requires:

- Blueprints – We must build according to the pattern of God's Word.
- Quality control – We don't just bring people in; we disciple them into maturity.

5. THE MISSION IS STILL THE GREAT COMMISSION

The heart of a Kingdom-minded leader beats with the mission of Christ:

"Go and make disciples of all nations . . ." (Matthew 28:19).

God's eternal purpose has always been to dwell among His people, and His Kingdom advances when we preach the Gospel, raise disciples, and build His Church with faithfulness and excellence.

REFLECTION
1. Is your life ruled by the King?
2. Are you building your own name or His Kingdom?
3. Do you live with the mindset of a Kingdom leader—someone who obeys Christ, builds the Church, and lives for transformation?

PRAYER

Father, thank You for making me part of Your Kingdom through Christ. Help me to live under Your rule, to be a faithful builder in Your Church, and to seek transformation wherever I go. Teach me to obey Your words and do Your works. Let my life and leadership glorify You and advance Your eternal purpose. In Jesus' name. Amen.

The Development of Gold Nuggets Through Your Life

51

Passing the Baton of Faith

"After that whole generation had been gathered to their ancestors, another generation grew up who knew neither the LORD nor what he had done for Israel" (Judges 2:10).

God thinks generationally. From Abraham to Isaac to Jacob, from Moses to Joshua, from Paul to Timothy—Scripture consistently shows that God's work doesn't end with one generation; it continues through the faithful passing of the baton.

Yet Judges 2:10 stands as a tragic warning: the baton was dropped. A whole generation "grew up who knew neither the Lord nor what He had done." That wasn't just failure, it was spiritual devastation.

1. HOW IS THE BATON BEING PASSED?

The baton is not just leadership—it is the Gospel. It is the knowledge of God, the testimony of His power, and the life of faith. We are each a runner in a race, and the next generation is already reaching back. What are we placing in their hands?

2. TODAY'S ALARMING REALITY

The image highlights the sobering statistics:
- South Korea, once a revival hotbed, now sees only 2.9% of the next generation identifying as Christian.
- Pew Research shows the median age of Christians is 30, while the median age of Muslims is 23—a stark reminder of the youth shift in spiritual identity.

This should awaken the Church. If we're not growing younger, we're not growing stronger.

3. GROWING YOUR CHURCH YOUNG

Reaching and retaining the next generation isn't a program—it's a priority. Churches that grow young do so by:
- Embracing intergenerational relationships.
- Giving real leadership opportunities to youth.
- Teaching timeless truth in a timely way.

Youth aren't just the Church of tomorrow—they're the Church of today.

4. UNDERSTANDING THE BATON

The baton we pass is more than theology—it's the lived Gospel, demonstrated in faith, obedience, love, and sacrifice. It's not just sermons but stories of God's faithfulness.

As Paul said, "What you have heard from me . . . entrust to reliable people who will also be qualified to teach others" (2 Timothy 2:2).

5. THE DANGER OF MOVING TOO FAST

In a relay race, speed without coordination causes disaster. We can run so fast with ministry plans, programs, and platforms that we drop the baton. We must slow down long enough to mentor, disciple, and transfer truth intentionally.

6. DON'T TAKE THE BATON TO THE GRAVE

We are guardians of this Gospel baton—but it was never meant to be buried with us.

Invest. Teach. Model. Release.

The next generation must know who God is—not just academically, but relationally and personally.

REFLECTION

1. Are you holding the baton with a tight grip, or are you preparing to pass it?
2. Who are you discipling?
3. Who is learning from your faith?

PRAYER

Lord, give us eyes to see the generation coming behind us. Help us not just to run faithfully but to pass the baton with wisdom and intentionality. Forgive us where we've failed to prepare others. Raise up a generation who knows You, loves You, and lives for Your glory. In Jesus' name. Amen.

52

Why We Give

"It is more blessed to give than to receive" (Acts 20:35).

"Give, and it will be given to you. A good measure, pressed down, shaken together and running over, will be poured into your lap" (Luke 6:38).

"Cast your bread upon the waters, for you will find it after many days" (Ecclesiastes 11:1, ESV).

Giving is more than a transaction—it's a revelation. It reveals our trust in God, our love for others, and the condition of our hearts. God does not need our money, but He does desire our hearts. And one of the clearest indicators of where our hearts are is in how we give.

1. IT IS MORE BLESSED TO GIVE THAN TO RECEIVE

Giving is a spiritual act that brings blessing not only to the recipient but also to the giver. It breaks selfishness, builds compassion, and opens us up to divine joy. When you give, you join in God's nature—because God is a giver.

2. THERE'S A PRINCIPLE OF RETURN

- "Cast your bread upon the waters . . ."
- "Give and it shall be given . . ."

These verses remind us that giving is like planting. What we release into God's hands doesn't disappear—it multiplies. While we don't give to get, we can expect God's faithfulness in return.

3. GIVING OPENS THE WINDOWS OF HEAVEN

Malachi 3 speaks of God pouring out blessings when we give with faith. Giving in obedience positions us under open heavens—where God's provision flows freely. It's not about obligation but invitation: Will you trust Me with what's in your hand?

4. WE GIVE BECAUSE GOD HAS BLESSED US

Everything we have is from Him. We are not owners, we are stewards. When we give, we acknowledge God as the Source of every good thing in our lives. Generosity is a response to grace.

5. GIVING REFLECTS THE CONDITION OF OUR HEART

Jesus said, "Where your treasure is, there your heart will be also" (Matthew 6:21).

We can sing, pray, and worship—but if we withhold our resources from God, it reveals a deeper resistance. True worship always includes surrendering, including financial surrender.

6. WE GIVE BECAUSE THE WORLD IS LOST

There are people who still need to hear the Gospel. Giving fuels missions, supports ministries, feeds the hungry, clothes the poor, and spreads the love of Christ. Every dollar surrendered can become a seed of eternal impact.

7. BECAUSE GOD EXPECTS IT

Giving is not optional, it's a command. God calls us to give generously, cheerfully, and consistently (2 Corinthians 9:7). It's part of discipleship. He expects it not out of compulsion, but from a heart that understands His generous love.

REFLECTION

1. Are you giving out of love or obligation?
2. Is your giving a true act of worship, or a leftover offering?

Ask God to help you see giving not as loss, but as investment into eternity.

PRAYER

Father, thank You for being the ultimate Giver. You gave Your Son so that we could have life. Teach me to give joyfully, faithfully, and generously. Let my giving reflect Your heart and help me trust You more deeply with all that I have. In Jesus' name. Amen.

53

Created with Purpose and Destiny

"Then God said, 'Let us make mankind in our image, in our likeness, so that they may rule . . .'" (Genesis 1:26).

"God blessed them and said to them, 'Be fruitful and increase in number; fill the earth and subdue it'" (Genesis 1:28).

From the very beginning, God created mankind not by accident, but with intention. You were never meant to live aimlessly. Your life has been stamped by the Creator with identity, authority, purpose, and blessing. These are not only ancient truths—they are foundational for how we are to live today.

1. IDENTITY – CREATED IN HIS IMAGE

God didn't make us like animals or angels—He made us like Himself. This is the root of our dignity, value, and uniqueness. Being made in His image means we reflect His nature, carry His creativity, and were designed for relationship with Him. Your identity begins not with what you do, but whose you are.

You are not what the world says about you. You are what God says about you: loved, chosen, and formed in His image.

2. AUTHORITY – DOMINION OVER THE EARTH

God entrusted humanity with stewardship over the earth. That means He gave us responsibility and influence. Our authority is not for control, but for care—to cultivate what God has given us and advance His purposes on the earth.

Spiritual authority begins with understanding that you were placed here on assignment.

3. PURPOSE – TENDING THE GARDEN

Even in paradise, Adam had a job to do. Work was not a punishment—it was part of his purpose. God designed us to contribute, to build, to protect, and to serve. When we align with God's purpose for our lives, our work becomes worship.

You were made to make a difference.

Your purpose is not found in busyness, but in faithfulness to the assignment God has given you.

4. BLESSING – EQUIPPED TO MULTIPLY

God didn't just give instructions—He gave empowerment. The first words spoken over mankind were a blessing: "Be fruitful and multiply." God blesses us not just to enjoy life, but to expand His Kingdom. His blessing enables us to thrive, not just survive.

When God blesses something, it grows. And He has blessed you.

REFLECTION

1. Are you walking in the fullness of what God gave at creation—identity, authority, purpose, and blessing?
2. Or have you allowed life, lies, or labels to cloud your view?

Take time today to reaffirm who you are in Him. You were made with divine intention. And He still has a plan for you.

PRAYER

Father, thank You for creating me with purpose. Thank You that I bear Your image, walk in Your authority, live with Your purpose, and carry Your blessing. Restore in me the truth of who I am in You. Help me live faithfully in alignment with Your design. In Jesus' name. Amen.

54

The Rhythm of Prayerful Living

"If any of you lacks wisdom, let him ask God, who gives generously to all without reproach, and it will be given him" (James 1:5, ESV).

"Be still, and know that I am God . . ." (Psalm 46:10).

"But be doers of the word, and not hearers only . . ." (James 1:22, ESV).

"Rejoice in the Lord always. I will say it again: Rejoice!" (Philippians 4:4).

In the busyness of life and the weight of uncertainty, God calls us to live in rhythm with Him. There is a divine flow in our relationship with Him—a spiritual pattern that keeps us grounded, guided, and growing. This rhythm includes five simple but powerful steps: Request, Relax, Receive, Respond, and Rejoice.

1. REQUEST

God invites us to bring our needs before Him. When we ask for wisdom and seek His will, we acknowledge His authority and our dependency.

Don't be afraid to ask. God delights in our asking when it's rooted in trust and surrender.

"Ask and it will be given to you . . ." (Matthew 7:7).

2. RELAX

After asking, we must rest. Rest in His sovereignty, His timing, His plan. Prayer is not panic—it's peace.

Trusting God means we stop striving to control what only He can.

"Cast all your anxiety on Him because He cares for you" (1 Peter 5:7).

3. RECEIVE

God is not silent. He speaks through His Word, His Spirit, His people, and even our circumstances. But we must be still and open to hear.

Don't rush the process. His voice often comes in the quiet, not the chaos.

"Speak, Lord, for Your servant is listening" (1 Samuel 3:10).

4. RESPOND

Hearing without obedience is disobedience. As God reveals His will, we must respond in faith, even when it's hard or uncertain.

Delayed obedience can be disobedience. Step forward when God speaks.

"Whatever He tells you, do it" (John 2:5).

5. REJOICE

Worship is not based on circumstances—it's based on who God is. We rejoice not just for what He has done, but for who He is: faithful, good, and present.

Joy is a weapon. Praise shifts the atmosphere of your heart and situation.

"Though the fig tree does not bud . . . yet I will rejoice in the LORD . . ." (Habakkuk 3:17–18).

REFLECTION

1. Are you living in the rhythm of God's presence and guidance?
2. Which step are you struggling most with right now?

Allow the Holy Spirit to walk you through each one. He is not in a hurry. He is with you in every part of the process.

PRAYER

Father, thank You for being near and attentive to my heart. Today, I bring my request before You. I choose to rest in Your control. Help me to receive Your wisdom, to respond with bold obedience, and to rejoice in every circumstance. You are good, and I trust You completely. In Jesus' name. Amen.

55

The God of Second Chances: Peter's Story

"Simon, son of John, do you love me? . . . Feed my sheep" (John 21:17).

"Being confident of this, that he who began a good work in you will carry it on to completion until the day of Christ Jesus" (Philippians 1:6).

Peter's story is one many of us can relate to: full of bold declarations, genuine love for Jesus—and painful failure. Yet it's also a story of restoration, grace, and renewed purpose. His life reminds us that failure is not final when God is involved.

1. PETER FAILED

Peter had promised Jesus unwavering loyalty: "Even if everyone else falls away—I never will!" (Mark 14:29). But when the moment of testing came, Peter didn't stand—he ran. He denied even knowing Jesus—not once, but three times.

We've all had moments when fear overpowered faith, or pride set us up for failure. But Jesus doesn't cancel us in our weakness—He meets us in it.

2. JESUS IS THE GOD OF SECOND CHANCES

After the resurrection, Jesus makes it a point to restore Peter:
- He sends a personal message: "Go tell the disciples and Peter . . ." (Mark 16:7).
- Peter runs to the empty tomb.
- Jesus appears to Peter personally (Luke 24:34).

- He prepares a meal for him and gently restores him with love and grace (John 21).
- He recommissions Peter: "Feed my sheep."

Jesus doesn't just forgive us—He restores us and reaffirms our calling.

3. PETER HAD TO RESPOND

Restoration is a gift, but it must be received. Peter had to:
- Accept Christ's love, even though he had failed.
- Accept His forgiveness, even though he didn't deserve it.
- Understand his new identity: not a denier, but a disciple empowered by Christ.
    - "Christ in me, the hope of glory" (Colossians 1:27).
    - The same Spirit that raised Jesus now lived in him.
- Trust in God's faithfulness: The One who called him would complete the work.
    - Jesus is the Alpha and the Omega—what He starts, He finishes.

REFLECTION

1. Where have you fallen short?
2. Are you still carrying shame from a past failure?

Peter's life proves that failure doesn't disqualify you, it can prepare you. God's grace is greater than your worst moment. Will you let Him restore you?

PRAYER

Lord Jesus, thank You that You are the God of second chances. Like Peter, I've failed You before—but I believe You haven't given up on me. Help me receive Your love and forgiveness, and to walk confidently in the purpose You've given me. I trust You to finish what You started in me. In Your name. Amen.

56

Training for Godliness

"Physical training is good, but training for godliness is much better, promising benefits in this life and in the life to come" (1 Timothy 4:8, NLT).

In a world that celebrates physical fitness, mental sharpness, and outward success, Paul reminds us of a deeper, more lasting pursuit—godliness.

Just as athletes train their bodies through discipline and dedication, we are called to train our hearts, minds, and spirits to reflect the character of Christ.

Physical exercise can strengthen the body, but spiritual exercise transforms the soul. Godliness is not about appearing religious—it's about becoming more like God in our thoughts, desires, and actions.

It is a life shaped by reverence for God and obedience to His Word.

WHAT IS GODLINESS?

Godliness means living in deep devotion to God, allowing His Spirit to shape every part of your life.

It is God-likeness—displaying His love, truth, mercy, and holiness in how you live each day.

It begins in the heart and is visible in how you respond to others, make decisions, and pursue what honors Him.

HOW TO TRAIN FOR GODLINESS

Training for godliness takes intentional effort and consistent practice. Here are a few ways to grow:

1. **Feed on the Word of God**. Make time daily to read, study, and meditate on Scripture. God's Word renews your mind and corrects your steps (2 Timothy 3:16–17).
2. **Strengthen Through Prayer**. Speak with God continually. Prayer deepens intimacy and aligns your will with His.
3. **Exercise Through Obedience**. Don't just hear the Word—do it. Each act of obedience strengthens your spiritual muscles.
4. **Join Spiritual Community**. Walk with other believers who will encourage and challenge your growth in faith.
5. **Practice Self-Discipline**. Say no to sin and distractions that weaken your focus on God. Fasting, simplicity, and generosity build godly character.

BENEFITS OF GODLINESS

Paul says godliness brings rewards now and forever.
In this life:
- Peace in the midst of chaos.
- Strength in weakness.
- Wisdom for daily living.
- Deep joy and contentment.

In the life to come:
- Eternal fellowship with God.
- Everlasting reward and rest in His presence.

Godliness carries eternal value. It shapes who you are becoming—not just for today, but for eternity.

REFLECTION

1. Where do you currently invest most of your energy—physical, mental, or spiritual growth? What does that reveal about your priorities?
2. In what ways do you see godliness as different from simply "being religious?" How would your life look if you pursued godliness with the same dedication an athlete gives to training?
3. When you examine your thoughts, desires, and actions, where do you see the likeness of Christ—and where is more formation needed?

4. How consistently do you "feed on the Word of God?" What helps you stay rooted in Scripture, and what obstacles tend to distract you?
5. Describe your current prayer life. How might deeper, more continual conversation with God shape your decisions and desires?

Training for godliness is a lifelong pursuit that shapes who you are today and who you will be for eternity. As you commit to these spiritual practices, may Christ be formed in you more fully, giving strength for this life and hope for the life to come.

PRAYER

Lord, help me to value what You value. Teach me to train my heart for godliness—to seek You first, to love what You love, and to walk in Your ways. May my life reflect Your goodness and truth, both now and forever. Amen.

57

Victory Over Fiery Darts

"Now the salvation, and the power, and the kingdom of our God and the authority of His Christ have come, for the accuser of our brethren has been thrown down, he who accuses them before our God day and night" (Revelation 12:10, NASB1995).

Each one of us is familiar with the voice of accusation, the internal voice that reminds us of our failures, magnifies our flaws, and tells us we're not good enough. According to Revelation 12:10, this is not merely psychological; it is deeply spiritual. Satan is called "the accuser of the brethren," and his mission is to relentlessly assault the minds and hearts of believers with lies.

But thanks be to God—there is hope, healing, and victory in Christ!

1. THE PURPOSE OF ACCUSATIONS

The enemy's accusations are never rooted in truth. John 8:44 reminds us that Satan is a liar and the father of lies. When he accuses us, his goal is to isolate, shame, and paralyze us spiritually. But accusations lose their power when exposed to the truth.

2. THE FIERY DARTS OF SATAN

In Zechariah 3, we see Satan accusing Joshua the high priest. Joshua stands in filthy garments, symbolizing sin, but God doesn't leave him there. The Lord rebukes Satan, removes the filthy clothes, and declares Joshua clean.

God doesn't just silence the accuser—He restores the accused. This is the picture of what Jesus has done for us:

- He took our sin (2 Corinthians 5:21).
- He became our Advocate (1 John 2:1).
- He is our righteousness.
- There is now no condemnation for those in Christ (Romans 8:1).

3. CONVICTION VS. CONDEMNATION

There is a difference between the Holy Spirit's conviction and Satan's accusation:

- Conviction leads to repentance and restoration.
- Accusation leads to shame and spiritual death.

As 2 Corinthians 7:10 says:

"Godly sorrow brings repentance that leads to salvation and leaves no regret, but worldly sorrow brings death."

The Holy Spirit points you to the cross. The accuser tries to keep you under it.

4. JESUS IS YOUR ADVOCATE

First John 2:2 declares that Jesus is the propitiation—the atoning sacrifice—for our sins. You don't have to defend yourself. Jesus already has. He is the advocate who stands in your defense, presenting not your performance, but His righteousness.

REFLECTION

1. Are you listening more to the voice of the accuser or the voice of your Advocate?
2. Are you living in shame, or are you walking in the righteousness Christ has given you?

PRAYER

Lord Jesus, thank You that You are my Advocate and Defender. I silence the voice of the accuser today and choose to stand in the truth of Your righteousness. Thank You for taking away my filthy garments and clothing me in Your grace. Help me to walk in freedom, not fear; in peace, not shame. In Your name. Amen.

58

Breaking Spiritual Bondages

"For though we walk in the flesh, we do not war after the flesh: (For the weapons of our warfare are not carnal, but mighty through God to the pulling down of strongholds." (2 Corinthians 10:3-4, KJV).

"So if the Son sets you free, you will be free indeed" (John 8:36).

Spiritual bondage is real—and it's not just a thing of the past or a problem in underdeveloped parts of the world. It's a present reality, even in modern, educated societies, and yes—even in the Church. Many believers suffer silently under spiritual bondage because of myths that must be broken by the light of God's truth.

1. EXPOSING THE MYTHS
- **Myth:** Demons only operated during Jesus' time.
- **Truth:** Ephesians 6:12 reminds us that we wrestle now against principalities and powers. The spiritual battle is ongoing.
- **Myth:** Christians are immune to demonic influence.
- **Truth:** While believers cannot be possessed, they can be oppressed, influenced, or entangled in spiritual bondage due to unaddressed sin, deception, or strongholds.

The first step to freedom is recognizing the reality of the battle.

2. UNDERSTANDING BONDAGE

Spiritual bondage isn't always dramatic. It can be subtle, hidden in the form of fear, depression, shame, or habitual sin. Bondage means the enemy has found a foothold in your life to oppress or influence you.

Three main types of bondage:

i. Ignorance, Deception, or Strongholds
When we don't know or live in the truth, the enemy exploits our ignorance (John 8:44).

ii. Legal Ground Through Unresolved Issues
These include:
- Unforgiveness
- Unconfessed sin
- Unholy soul ties (1 Corinthians 6:16)
- Cursed or unclean objects (Deuteronomy 7:26)
- Spoken curses or negative words (Proverbs 18:21)
- Generational sins (Exodus 20:5)
- Unholy vows or oaths

iii. Direct Demonic Influence
The Bible shows how Satan influenced David (1 Chronicles 21:1), Judas (John 13:2), and Ananias (Acts 5:3). If it happened then, it can happen now.

3. THE PATH TO FREEDOM

Deliverance doesn't come through religious routine or good behavior—it comes through a power encounter with Jesus Christ. His authority breaks every chain.

Freedom begins with:
- Repentance – A turning away from sin and a turning to God.
- Renunciation – Verbally rejecting every foothold you've allowed the enemy to have.
- Renewal – Replacing lies with truth and walking in the power of the Holy Spirit.

Jesus didn't just save us from sin—He saved us to walk in freedom.

REFLECTION

1. Are there areas in your life where you feel stuck, defeated, or spiritually oppressed?

Ask the Holy Spirit to reveal any hidden bondage and invite Jesus to set you free.

PRAYER

Lord Jesus, You are the Deliverer. I confess any area of my life where I've given the enemy access—whether through sin, ignorance, or wounds. I renounce every lie, every curse, and every chain in Jesus' name. Set me free by Your power and fill me with Your Spirit. I choose to walk in truth, freedom, and victory. In Your name. Amen.

59

The Battle of a Doubtful Mind

"But when you ask, you must believe and not doubt, because the one who doubts is like a wave of the sea, blown and tossed by the wind. That person should not expect to receive anything from the Lord. Such a person is double-minded and unstable in all they do" (James 1:6–8).

Life's greatest battles are often fought not in the world around us, but in the arena of our minds. James speaks directly to this internal war, warning us about the danger of a doubtful and double-minded spirit. Doubt can erode faith, disorient our direction, and disrupt our peace.

1. WHAT IS DOUBT?

Doubt is more than hesitation—it is a thought in opposition to God's Word and promises. While faith is born in the spirit and anchored in God, doubt originates in the mind and is fueled by reason, fear, and uncertainty.

When we doubt, we're not just unsure—we're choosing to lean on our own understanding rather than trusting in God's.

"Trust in the Lord with all your heart and do not lean on your own understanding" (Proverbs 3:5).

2. REASON VS. FAITH

There are two forces constantly at work in our lives:

- **Reason:** Lives in the mind, depends on logic, and demands to understand before obeying.
- **Faith:** Operates in the spirit, trusts God's voice, and obeys even when it doesn't make sense.

Peter exemplifies this in Matthew 14. He had enough faith to step out of the boat—but when he shifted his focus to the storm, reason overtook faith, and he began to sink.

Jesus didn't rebuke Peter for walking on water—He questioned why he doubted after already experiencing the power of faith.

3. FAITH IS A GIFT AND A KEY

Romans 12:3 reminds us that God gives each of us a measure of faith. That faith must be used, fed, and protected. Hebrews 11:6 tells us it is impossible to please God without faith, because faith is the currency of relationship with Him—it affirms that He exists and that He rewards those who diligently seek Him.

4. THE DANGER OF A DOUBLE MIND

A double-minded person is divided—torn between trusting God and trusting self. This instability blocks the flow of wisdom, peace, and answered prayer. God desires our whole heart—not a divided one.

Doubt creates delay. Faith produces movement.

REFLECTION

1. Are you living in faith or dominated by doubt?
2. Are you leaning more on your understanding or on God's promises?
3. What area of your life do you need to surrender in full trust today?

PRAYER

Lord, I confess that I've let doubt rule my mind at times. Forgive me for being double-minded. Today I choose to trust You with all my heart. Help me to silence doubt with Your Word and strengthen my faith through Your Spirit. I declare that my mind belongs to You, and I will walk by faith, not by sight. In Jesus' name. Amen.

60

The Power of Forgiveness

"Do not take revenge, my dear friends, but leave room for God's wrath, for it is written: 'It is mine to avenge; I will repay,' says the Lord" (Romans 12:19).

"Be kind and compassionate to one another, forgiving each other, just as in Christ God forgave you" (Ephesians 4:32).

Forgiveness is one of the most challenging commands of the Christian life—and yet, it is one of the most liberating. It is not about forgetting the pain or excusing the offense. It's about choosing to release the debt and walking into the freedom God has for you.

1. FORGIVENESS IS A CHOICE, NOT A FEELING

If you wait to feel like forgiving, you may never get there. Forgiveness begins with a decision of the will. It's not about pretending the pain didn't happen—it's about refusing to let that pain hold you captive any longer.

"Forgive in order to heal." We don't wait to be healed to forgive; we forgive to start the healing process.

2. FORGIVENESS FREES YOU, NOT JUST THE OFFENDER

Unforgiveness is a prison, but the only person behind the bars is you. When you release someone from your personal judgment, you're not saying what they did was right. You're saying you're done carrying the weight.

"To forgive is to set a captive free, and then realize you were the captive" (Lewis B. Smedes).

3. YOU ARE LETTING THEM OFF YOUR HOOK, NOT GOD'S

Romans 12:19 reminds us: vengeance belongs to God. Forgiveness does not mean justice is ignored. It means you are trusting God to deal with the offense in His perfect wisdom and timing.

4. FORGIVENESS IS LIVING WITH THE CONSEQUENCES—IN FREEDOM

We all live with the consequences of others' sin, but we get to choose whether we carry that burden with bitterness or with freedom. Forgiveness says, "I won't keep rehearsing your offense. I choose peace."

Bitter people rehearse the pain. Forgiven people release it.

5. DO NOT WAIT—ACT ON FORGIVENESS TODAY

- Don't wait until it feels right.
- Don't hold on to the pain until it breaks you.
- Don't give Satan a foothold through your bitterness.
- Do forgive from the heart.

And when seeking forgiveness from others:

- Own your wrong without excuses.
- Don't shift the blame.
- Don't rely on texts or emails—be humble and present.

REFLECTION

1. Is there someone you need to forgive?
2. Or someone from whom you need to seek forgiveness?
3. Are you holding on to bitterness that's keeping you in bondage?

PRAYER

Lord, I thank You for the forgiveness You've shown me through Christ. Help me to choose forgiveness, even when it's hard. I release the hurt, the offense, and the right to revenge. Set me free from the prison of bitterness, and teach me to walk in the healing and peace that comes through grace. In Jesus' name. Amen.

61

Walking in Freedom

"For though we walk in the flesh, we do not war after the flesh: (For the weapons of our warfare are not carnal, but mighty through God to the pulling down of strong holds)" (2 Corinthians 10:3–4, KJV).

You were not created to live in bondage. You were created to walk in freedom. But freedom doesn't happen by accident; it requires intentional, spiritual warfare. The battleground is not your past, your circumstances, or even the people around you. The true battleground is your mind.

1. WE ARE IN A BATTLE

Paul makes it clear: we wrestle not against flesh and blood (Ephesians 6:12). The war is real—and Satan's strategy is to trap us through:

- Lies
- Deceptions
- Temptations
- Accusations

His goal? To keep you bound—to your past, to shame, to fear, and to false identities.

The enemy cannot steal your salvation, but he'll do everything to paralyze your purpose.

2. VICTORY REQUIRES A CHOICE

You must choose to win. Freedom starts with replacing lies with God's truth.

- Believing a lie empowers the liar.

- What you believe will shape how you live—even if it's not true.
- The devil doesn't need a prison if he can deceive you into thinking you're already trapped.

Romans 12:2 tells us that transformation happens by the renewing of your mind. If your thoughts don't change, your life won't change.

3. YOUR PAST DOESN'T DEFINE YOUR FUTURE

Israel had been set free from Egypt, but Egypt was still in their mindset. They were out of slavery, but slavery was not out of them. As a result, they longed for what had once oppressed them (Numbers 11:5–6).

Don't frame your future through the lens of your past.

God has a Promised Land ahead of you, but you must leave the bondage of Egypt behind you—mentally and spiritually.

4. CHANGE YOUR PERSPECTIVE THROUGH PRAYER AND PRAISE

If it's big enough to worry about, it's big enough to pray about. If it's on your mind, it's already on God's heart.

"Cast all your cares on Him, for He cares for you" (1 Peter 5:7).

Prayer and praise are powerful weapons. They shift your focus, align your heart with truth, and invite the presence of God into your battle.

REFLECTION

1. Are there lies you've been believing about your identity, your past, or your future?
2. Are you walking in freedom or still thinking like a captive?
3. Are you renewing your mind daily with God's truth?

PRAYER

Lord, I thank You that I was not created to live in bondage but in freedom. I choose today to reject every lie of the enemy and to renew my mind with Your Word. Deliver me from the Egypt of my past and help me to think like a child of promise. I cast my cares on You, knowing that You care for me. In Jesus' name. Amen.

62

Replacing Lies with Truth

"You will know the truth, and the truth will set you free" (John 8:32).

"When he lies, he speaks his native language, for he is a liar and the father of lies" (John 8:44).

"Whatever is true . . . think about such things" (Philippians 4:8).

We are living in the midst of a spiritual battle—and the battlefield is the mind. Satan, described by Jesus as "the father of lies," doesn't need chains to bind us; all he needs is a convincing lie. A lie believed as truth will affect your life as if it were true—even when it's not.

1. THE STRATEGY OF THE ENEMY

Satan has no real power over the believer except deception. From the garden of Eden to the wilderness temptation of Jesus, he has always used lies to twist God's Word, plant doubt, and distort reality.

If Satan can control your thoughts, he can control your direction.

2. COMMON LIES WE BELIEVE

- "God can't forgive me."
- "I'll never be free from this struggle."
- "I'm not enough."
- "God has forgotten me."

These are not just thoughts—they are weapons aimed at your identity and purpose. When you agree with a lie, you empower the liar.

3. THE EFFECTS OF BELIEVING LIES

- Anxiety grows.

- Peace disappears.
- Faith weakens.
- Purpose fades.

Your life tends to move in the direction of your strongest thoughts. That's why the Word of God calls us to "take every thought captive to make it obedient to Christ" (2 Corinthians 10:5).

4. THE POWER OF TRUTH

Truth isn't just a concept—it's a Person. Jesus declared, "I am the way, the truth, and the life" (John 14:6). The more we renew our minds with the Word of God, the more lies are exposed, and the more freedom we walk in.

Philippians 4:8–9 gives us the strategy:
- Think about what is true.
- Put it into practice.
- Experience the peace of God.

This is the pattern: Thought → Action → Experience.

5. FREEDOM REQUIRES CONFRONTATION

You cannot change what you do not confront. The first step to freedom is recognizing lies. Then, remove it and replace it with God's truth.

Every time you confront a lie with the truth, you reclaim ground the enemy tried to steal.

REFLECTION

1. What lies have you allowed into your thinking?
2. What is God's truth that replaces that lie?
3. How can you renew your mind daily with the truth of Scripture?

PRAYER

Father, I recognize that the enemy has tried to plant lies in my heart and mind. Today, I reject every lie and ask You to replace it with Your truth. Help me to think on what is true, noble, right, and pure. I choose to renew my mind with Your Word and walk in the freedom You have promised. In Jesus' name. Amen.

63

The Mind of Christ

"Let this mind be in you, which was also in Christ Jesus . . ." (Philippians 2:5, KJV).

The Christian life is not simply about believing in Jesus—it's about becoming like Him. Paul calls us to let the same mind that was in Christ be in us. That means adopting not just His mission, but His mindset—how He thought, lived, and responded. This transformation begins in the battlefield of the mind.

1. A SUBMISSIVE MIND

Jesus submitted fully to the will of the Father. He didn't act independently but said, "I have come down from heaven not to do my will but to do the will of him who sent me" (John 6:38).

Even in suffering, "He learned obedience by the things which He suffered" (Hebrews 5:8).

A mind like Christ's starts with surrender. True freedom is found in obedience to God's will.

2. A HUMBLE MIND

Jesus humbled Himself—not just at the cross, but from His birth to His daily life. He embraced poverty, served the unworthy, and endured injustice without retaliation.

Humility isn't weakness—it's strength under submission.

"He made Himself of no reputation . . . and became obedient unto death—even the death of the cross" (Philippians 2:7–8).

3. A SERVANT MIND

Jesus didn't come to be served but to serve (Mark 10:45). He washed feet, welcomed children, healed the broken, and touched the untouchable. His greatness was found in serving.

If we want the mind of Christ, we must let go of entitlement and take up the towel of servanthood.

4. A SACRIFICIAL MIND

Christ bore our sins—He gave His life so that we might live. His thoughts were not consumed with self-preservation but with self-giving love.

"God made him who had no sin to be sin for us . . ."
(2 Corinthians 5:21)

" . . . that we might become the righteousness of God."

A Christ-like mind is willing to give, even when it costs.

5. BECOMING LIKE CHRIST

How do we develop the mind of Christ?
- Renew your mind daily with God's Word (Romans 12:2).
- Surrender your will in prayer (Luke 22:42).
- Walk in humility and dependence on the Holy Spirit.
- Serve others intentionally and sacrificially.
- Choose obedience even when it's difficult.

REFLECTION

1. Do your thoughts reflect the humility, submission, and service of Christ?
2. What area of your mindset needs to come under the Lordship of Jesus today?

PRAYER

Lord Jesus, I want to think, live, and love like You. Transform my mind. Teach me humility, surrender, and the joy of serving others. Help me to reject selfish ambition and to pursue Your will above all else. I surrender my thoughts and desires to You. Give me the mind of Christ. In Your name. Amen.

64

Overcoming Flesh Patterns

"Do not conform to the pattern of this world, but be transformed by the renewing of your mind" (Romans 12:2).

"Whatever you have learned or received or heard from me, or seen in me—put it into practice. And the God of peace will be with you" (Philippians 4:9).

Every believer has two realities: a new identity in Christ, and an old habit-forming residue called the flesh. When we are born again, we become new creations in spirit, but our minds and emotions may still carry old patterns—ways of reacting, coping, and thinking that were formed before Christ.

These are what we call flesh patterns.

1. THE REALITY OF RESIDUE

Your conversion changed your position before God, but it didn't automatically delete the patterns formed in your past. Memories, wounds, and habits still exist. Many Christians struggle because they try to live the new life while still walking in the patterns of the old.

You cannot cast out what needs to be crucified. Flesh patterns don't leave by command—they must be overcome by truth.

2. FLESH MUST BE REPLACED, NOT MANAGED

Managing the flesh leads to frustration. Overcoming it requires:

- Renewing the mind (Romans 12:2).
- Thinking differently (Philippians 4:8).
- Living out truth daily (Philippians 4:9).

Flesh thrives where truth is absent. It dies when truth is practiced.

3. IDENTIFYING AND RESOLVING INNER CONFLICTS

Before we can truly live free, we must deal with what hinders our relationship with God:
- **Rebellion (1 Samuel 15:23):** Resisting God's authority keeps us stuck.
- **Pride (James 4:6):** Independence from God blocks grace.
- **Bitterness and Unforgiveness (Matthew 18:34):** Resentment poisons peace.

These are not just emotions, they are strongholds. And until they're confronted, peace remains elusive.

4. THE PATHWAY TO FREEDOM

Overcoming flesh patterns is not a one-time event but a spiritual journey marked by intentional choices:
- Believe the truth about who God is and who you are in Him.
- Confess areas of sin and struggle honestly before God.
- Renounce the lies and vows you've made in the flesh.
- Forgive those who have wounded you; release them to release yourself.

Deliverance begins with decision. Transformation happens through daily submission.

REFLECTION

1. Are there any flesh patterns you keep repeating?
2. Have you resolved rebellion, pride, or unforgiveness in your heart?
3. Are you actively renewing your mind with God's Word?

PRAYER

Father, I recognize that there are still patterns in me that do not reflect You. I confess any rebellion, pride, and bitterness. Today I choose truth over feelings, freedom over bondage, and Your Word over my wounds. Renew my mind, heal my heart, and help me walk fully in the Spirit. In Jesus' name. Amen.

65

Steps to Freedom

"Then you will know the truth, and the truth will set you free" (John 8:32).

"It is for freedom that Christ has set us free. Stand firm, then, and do not let yourselves be burdened again by a yoke of slavery" (Galatians 5:1).

Many Christians live saved but not free. Though redeemed by the blood of Christ, they find themselves trapped in patterns of fear, shame, guilt, and self-condemnation. Why? Because freedom requires more than forgiveness—it requires transformation.

Freedom doesn't come by accident. It follows a deliberate path—a journey into truth and away from deception.

1. ASSUME RESPONSIBILITY FOR YOUR OWN ACTIONS AND ATTITUDES

The first step to freedom is ownership. You cannot blame others for what only you can surrender. True freedom begins when you stop pointing outward and start looking inward.

God's grace empowers us to change, but He will not force us to choose.

2. REMOVE LIES AND REPLACE THEM WITH TRUTH

Satan's most effective weapons are lies. When we believe his accusations, temptations, or deceptions, we give him influence. You don't fight lies with feelings—you fight them with truth.

- Identify what lies you've believed:
  - "I'm not enough."
  - "God can't forgive me."
  - "Things will never change."

- Replace them with God's truth:
  - "I am a new creation" (2 Corinthians 5:17).
  - "There is no condemnation for those in Christ" (Romans 8:1).

Truth is not just information—it's the weapon that sets you free.

3. IDENTIFY AND REMOVE DECEPTION IN YOUR LIFE

Deception thrives where there is ignorance or pride. Ask the Holy Spirit to reveal blind spots—areas where you've allowed compromise, false beliefs, or hidden sin to take root.

"Search me, O God, and know my heart..." (Psalm 139:23).

When deception is uncovered, don't justify it. Repent and realign your heart with the Word of God.

4. WALK IN THE SPIRIT DAILY

Freedom is not a one-time experience; it's a lifestyle. Keep in step with the Spirit through daily surrender, prayer, and Scripture. You can't live a free life on yesterday's decision—you must choose Christ today and every day.

Freedom isn't just the absence of bondage—it's the presence of Jesus ruling your heart and mind.

REFLECTION

1. Are there lies you've believed that are keeping you bound?
2. Have you taken full responsibility for your spiritual condition?
3. What truth do you need to replace deception with today?

PRAYER

Father, thank You for calling me to freedom. I confess the ways I've given room to the enemy through lies and deception. Today, I take responsibility for my heart, and I choose Your truth over every lie. Help me walk in the Spirit and live in the liberty Christ died to give me. In Jesus' name. Amen.

66

Overcoming Temptation

"No temptation has overtaken you except what is common to mankind. And God is faithful; He will not let you be tempted beyond what you can bear. But when you are tempted, He will also provide a way out so that you can endure it" (1 Corinthians 10:13).

Temptation is a universal experience. Whether you are a new believer or a seasoned follower of Christ, you will face the pull of the flesh, the pressure of the world, and the subtle whispers of the enemy. But Scripture reminds us that temptation is not sin—yielding to it is. And through Christ, we are given the power to overcome.

1. THE SOURCE OF TEMPTATION

Temptation doesn't begin after conversion—it begins at birth. It is rooted in our fallen nature. After salvation, we receive a new spirit, but our minds and flesh still carry old patterns and memories.

We must intentionally:
- Renew our minds (Romans 12:2).
- Put on the mind of Christ (Philippians 2:5).
- Live by the Spirit, not the flesh (Galatians 5:16).

Salvation is the starting point of freedom, not the finish line.

2. CHANNELS OF TEMPTATION – 1 JOHN 2:15–17

Temptation usually comes through three channels:
- Lust of the flesh – Desires that seek gratification without God.
- Lust of the eyes – Cravings for what looks good but may not be godly.
- Pride of life – Seeking identity and worth apart from God.

These were the very channels Satan used in the Garden, in the wilderness with Jesus, and still uses today.

We don't resist temptation by willpower—we overcome by truth, dependence on the Holy Spirit, and wisdom.

3. LEVELS OF SPIRITUAL MATURITY – 1 JOHN 2:12–14

John outlines a growth process:

- Little children – Know forgiveness and salvation (penalty of sin is broken).
- Young men – Learn to overcome the enemy (power of sin is broken).
- Fathers – Know God intimately (presence of sin loses its grip).

Spiritual maturity is measured not just by knowledge but by our ability to walk in victory over temptation.

4. VICTORY OVER TEMPTATION

- Recognize the lie in every temptation. Satan always distorts truth.
- Replace the lie with Scripture. Jesus overcame by saying, "It is written . . ."
- Rely on the Holy Spirit. He gives discernment, strength, and escape.
- Resist actively. Don't entertain or negotiate with temptation—flee from it (2 Timothy 2:22).
- Restore quickly. If you fall, confess immediately. God's mercy renews.

There is always a way out. God is faithful to provide it.

REFLECTION

1. What patterns from your past still tempt you today?
2. Are you daily renewing your mind and depending on the Spirit?
3. Which channel (flesh, eyes, pride) do you struggle with most?

PRAYER

Lord, I thank You that no temptation is too strong for Your grace. Teach me to recognize the enemy's lies and to overcome with Your truth. Help me to grow in spiritual maturity, to walk by the Spirit, and to live in daily victory. Strengthen me when I am weak, and remind me that You are faithful to deliver me. In Jesus' name. Amen.

67

Battlefield of the Mind

"Now may the God of peace Himself sanctify you entirely; and may your spirit and soul and body be preserved complete, without blame at the coming of our Lord Jesus Christ" (1 Thessalonians 5:23, NASB1995).

"Do not conform to the pattern of this world, but be transformed by the renewing of your mind" (Romans 12:2).

The greatest spiritual battles often take place in the quiet space between your ears—your mind. While the spirit connects us to God and the body interacts with the world, the soul—comprising your mind, will, and emotions—is where choices are made, thoughts are formed, and peace or turmoil is determined.

The battlefield of the mind is where victory is either seized or surrendered.

1. THE MIND: THE INTERSECTION OF SPIRIT AND BODY

According to 1 Corinthians 2:11, no one knows the thoughts of a person but their own spirit—and no one knows God's thoughts but His Spirit. Your mind has the unique role of choosing daily whether to follow the voice of your flesh or the leading of the Spirit.

Your body is not in control of your mind; your mind must rule over your body—by aligning with the Spirit.

2. THE ANXIOUS AND WORRIED MIND

Jesus addressed anxiety in Matthew 6:30–33, showing that worry grows when we underestimate the power of God and overestimate the value of things.

- When we worry, we are acting like orphans instead of children of a Father who knows our needs.
- An anxious mind forgets that God is both sovereign and faithful.

Worry thrives where trust is absent.

3. HOW THE MIND AFFECTS THE WHOLE PERSON

As Dr. Herbert Benson stated, the mind and body communicate constantly. What you think, perceive, and meditate on directly influences your physical, emotional, and spiritual health.

- Fear increases cortisol.
- Hope boosts resilience.
- Gratitude activates peace.
- Truth transforms your entire being.

What you feed your mind, you feed your life.

4. CULTIVATING THE MIND OF CHRIST

Philippians 2:5 says, "Let this mind be in you which was also in Christ Jesus."

How do we cultivate a Spirit-led mind?

- Saturate your thoughts with Scripture.
- Submit your will to God daily.
- Sift your emotions through truth, not feelings.
- Silence lies with worship and prayer.

The more you choose truth, the more your mind becomes a gateway of peace instead of a war zone of fear.

REFLECTION

1. Are you feeding your mind with truth or with fear?
2. What thoughts dominate your inner life—faith or worry?
3. How can you realign your mind today to walk in peace?

PRAYER

Lord, I surrender my mind to You today. I repent for giving space to worry, fear, and lies. Renew my thoughts and help me take every thought captive to the obedience of Christ. Let my mind be a place where truth reigns, where Your Spirit leads, and where peace lives. In Jesus' name. Amen.

68

Healing the Wounds Within

"He heals the brokenhearted and binds up their wounds" (Psalm 147:3).

"The Spirit of the Lord GOD is upon me . . . He has sent me to bind up the brokenhearted, to proclaim freedom for the captives . . ." (Isaiah 61:1, NASB1995).

Every one of us carries a trauma profile—wounds from the past, scars from betrayal, abuse, failure, abandonment, or rejection. They may be buried beneath the surface, but they shape how we think, how we react, and how we relate to others. Unhealed wounds become strongholds in the mind, and they can imprison the soul.

Yet God's heart has always been to heal the broken, set the captive free, and bind up the wounded. That healing starts when we stop ignoring the pain and start inviting God into it.

1. ACKNOWLEDGE THE WOUND

Out of sight doesn't mean out of mind. That thing you don't want to talk about, think about, or face is likely the thing causing the most spiritual damage.

What you hide, the enemy uses. What you expose, God heals.

Psalm 142:7 cries out: "Bring my soul out of prison, that I may praise your name."

2. CLEANSE THE WOUND

Healing begins with confession and forgiveness.
- "If we confess our sins, He is faithful and just to forgive us . . ." (1 John 1:9).
- Forgiveness is not just for others, it's for you.

- It purges bitterness, guilt, and self-pity.

You cannot walk in freedom while holding onto resentment. Forgiveness is the doorway to healing.

3. PROTECT THE WOUND

Once the wound is cleansed, it must be protected with truth.

Romans 12:2 commands us to renew our minds. Why? Because the enemy seeks to reinfect you with lies:

- "You'll never heal."
- "You deserved the pain."
- "God has forgotten you."

Reject the lies. Guard your heart with God's truth. Don't dwell on the wound—declare the Word.

4. MONITOR THE WOUND

First Peter 5:8 warns us to be sober and vigilant. Even healed areas can become vulnerable if not guarded. The enemy is relentless, but God is greater.

Keep watch over your soul. Stay in prayer. Stay in the Word. Stay in community.

REFLECTION

1. What wounds have you hidden that God is asking you to expose today?
2. Who do you need to forgive to move toward healing?
3. What lie have you believed that needs to be replaced with God's truth?

PRAYER

Father, I bring my wounded heart before You. I confess that I have hidden pain and held onto bitterness. Today I choose to forgive. I receive Your forgiveness and healing. Renew my mind with Your truth, and help me guard my heart. I believe You are the God who heals, and I surrender every wound to You. In Jesus' name. Amen.

69

Breaking My Alabaster Jar

"Then Mary took about a pint of pure nard, an expensive perfume; she poured it on Jesus' feet and wiped his feet with her hair. And the house was filled with the fragrance of the perfume" (John 12:3).

In a moment of pure devotion, Mary broke her alabaster jar—a costly container filled with perfume—and anointed the feet of Jesus. What looked extravagant to others was, to her, an offering of love, sacrifice, and worship. This act holds profound lessons for anyone who desires to love Jesus deeply.

1. EXTRAVAGANT LOVE

Mary's act revealed the depth of her gratitude. Jesus had forgiven her, restored her brother Lazarus, and transformed her life. She didn't just pour out perfume—she poured out her heart.

"He who has been forgiven much, loves much" (Luke 7:47).

Real worship is not casual—it's costly. True love for Jesus will always find a way to be expressed in sacrificial devotion.

2. COSTLY SACRIFICE

This alabaster jar represented a year's wages—possibly even her dowry, her future. When Mary broke it, she held nothing back. She gave all she had, and once poured out, there was no taking it back.

"I will not offer to the Lord that which costs me nothing" (2 Samuel 24:24).

Like the widow who gave her last two coins (Luke 21:1–4), Mary's worship wasn't measured by how much she gave, but by how much she had left—and she held nothing in reserve.

3. THE FRAGRANCE OF WORSHIP

Her sacrifice didn't just bless Jesus—it changed the atmosphere. Scripture says the house was filled with the fragrance of her offering. Worship is contagious. When we pour out our love for Jesus, others are drawn into His presence.

- Worship brings the focus back to Jesus.
- Worship opens hearts.
- Worship shifts rooms.

4. SEIZING THE MOMENT

Mary's worship was timely. While others waited, she acted. She didn't postpone her offering. Later, when others came with spices to anoint Jesus' body (Mark 16:1), it was too late—He had already risen.

Worship delayed is worship missed.

Don't wait for the "right time"—now is the moment to pour out your praise.

REFLECTION

1. What does your alabaster jar represent?
2. Are you holding back any part of your love or devotion to Jesus?
3. What "fragrance" does your worship bring into your home, church, or community?

PRAYER

Lord Jesus, You are worthy of everything I have. Teach me to worship like Mary—with boldness, with sacrifice, and with love that holds nothing back. Help me to seize every moment to honor You and fill every place I go with the fragrance of true worship. I break my alabaster jar at Your feet today. In Your name. Amen.

70

Does God Still Heal?

"Jesus reached out his hand and touched the man. 'I am willing,' he said. 'Be clean!' Immediately he was cleansed of his leprosy" (Matthew 8:3).

" . . . but just say the word, and my servant will be healed" (Matthew 8:8).

One of the timeless questions many people carry in their hearts is, "Does God still heal?" The answer found in Scripture is clear—not only can He heal, but He is willing to heal. Healing is not just what Jesus did; it's who He is—Jehovah Rapha, the Lord who heals.

In Matthew 8, we find two powerful examples: the leper and the centurion. Their encounters with Jesus reveal a pattern of approaching God that still holds power today.

1. WORSHIP FIRST

The leper came and worshipped Jesus before presenting his need (Matthew 8:2). Even in his physical suffering, he recognized Jesus as Lord.

Before you ask for healing, acknowledge the Healer.

Worship aligns our hearts with God's presence. It shifts the focus from our condition to His compassion.

2. BRING YOUR NEED HONESTLY

The leper said, "If You are willing, You can make me clean." This was not doubt—it was reverence. He recognized Jesus' power and submitted to His will.

Faith is not demanding—it is trusting in God's sovereignty and mercy.

Bring your needs boldly but humbly. You can be honest with God about your pain and still trust His process.

3. BELIEVE IN HIS WILLINGNESS

Jesus responded with a touch and a declaration: "I will; be clean." He didn't hesitate. He didn't rebuke. He responded.

God is not only able—He is willing. His heart is for wholeness.

4. EXERCISE FAITH LIKE THE CENTURION

The centurion came to Jesus not for himself, but for another. He understood the power of authority and believed that Jesus' word alone was enough.

"Speak the word only . . ."—this is the language of true faith.

Jesus marveled at the centurion's faith. This man didn't need a sign—just a promise.

5. APPLICATION FOR US TODAY

From these accounts, we learn a practical spiritual posture when seeking healing:

- Come to Jesus – Don't isolate your pain. Bring it into His presence.
- Worship Jesus – Lift your eyes above the affliction.
- Recognize Jesus as Lord – Healing flows from authority.
- Make your request known – Don't be silent in your suffering.
- Exercise faith – Trust that even a word from Jesus is enough.

REFLECTION

1. Are you seeking healing today—in body, soul, or mind?
2. Have you come into God's presence with worship and faith?
3. Are you willing to trust His timing, His way, and His heart?

PRAYER

Lord Jesus, I come to You as the Healer and Restorer. I worship You not just for what You can do, but for who You are. I present my needs to You, trusting in Your perfect will and loving heart. Speak the word, and let healing flow—whether physically, emotionally, or spiritually. I believe You are able, and I believe You are willing. In Jesus' name. Amen.

71

Equipped to Serve

"You, my brothers and sisters, were called to be free. But do not use your freedom to indulge the flesh; rather, serve one another humbly in love" (Galatians 5:13).

We are not saved to sit—we are saved to serve. The Christian life is not simply about attending church or growing spiritually for our own sake; it is about becoming the hands and feet of Jesus to a world in need. Freedom in Christ is not a license for self-indulgence—it's a platform for humble service.

1. JESUS MODELED SERVANTHOOD

In John 13, Jesus—Lord and Teacher—stooped low and washed His disciples' feet. He didn't just teach servanthood; He demonstrated it.

"I have set you an example that you should do as I have done for you" (John 13:15).

Greatness in the Kingdom is measured not by how many serve you, but by how well you serve others (Matthew 20:26).

2. WE ARE GIFTED TO SERVE

God never calls us without equipping us. First Peter 4:10–11 reminds us that every believer has received a gift—something unique to contribute to the body of Christ.

Your gift is not for your glory, but for God's glory and others' good.

When we speak, serve, teach, or encourage, we do it with the strength God provides. That means no one is unqualified in His eyes.

3. WE ARE BLESSED TO SERVE

Luke 12:48 reminds us that much is required of those to whom much has been given. We are not owners—we are stewards. Every resource, skill, and opportunity is entrusted to us to be used in love.

Serving is not a burden, it's a blessing.

When you serve others, you become the answer to someone's prayer.

4. LOVE COMPELS US TO SERVE

True service is birthed from love. First Peter 4:8–9 challenges us to love deeply and offer hospitality without grumbling. Love doesn't wait for perfect conditions or ideal timing—it moves into action.

Love doesn't look for excuses—it looks for opportunities.

5. SILENCING THE EXCUSES

Many say:
- "I don't have time."
- "I'm not gifted enough."
- "They don't need me."

But here's the truth: God does not call the equipped—He equips the called.

If He has placed a burden in your heart, He will place the tools in your hand.

REFLECTION

1. Where is God calling you to serve in this season?
2. What gifts or passions has He entrusted to you for others' benefit?
3. What excuses do you need to surrender today?

PRAYER

Lord, thank You for calling me to serve. Forgive me for the times I've hesitated, doubted, or held back. Help me to serve with humility, love, and joy. Let my life be a reflection of Your grace at work. Show me where and how to use my gifts for Your glory and others' good. In Jesus' name. Amen.

72

Abraham's Journey of Faith

"The LORD had said to Abram, 'Go from your country, your people and your father's household to the land I will show you'" (Genesis 12:1).

Abraham's story begins with one simple, yet life-altering word from God: "Go." It was a divine command that uprooted his entire life and placed him on the path to becoming the father of faith. His journey was not about knowing every detail—it was about trusting the One who called him.

1. A CALL OUT OF COMFORT

God called Abraham while he was still in Mesopotamia (Acts 7:2–3)—in the midst of familiar surroundings, family, and traditions. The command was clear: "Leave your land, your relatives, and your father's house."

Faith often begins with letting go.

We, too, are called out of comfort zones, habits, and worldly patterns. Following God will cost us something—but it will never cost us more than what we gain in Him.

2. A JOURNEY WITHOUT ALL THE DETAILS

Abraham was called to a land that God "would show him." There was no map, no GPS, no timeline—just a promise.

Real faith says yes before all the details are known.

Like Abraham, we must learn to trust the Guide more than the route.

3. A LIFE ANCHORED IN PROMISE

God didn't just call Abraham out—He called him into something greater:

- Progeny – "I will make you a great nation"
- Prominence – "I will make your name great"
- Protection – "I will bless those who bless you . . ."
- Purpose – "All peoples on earth will be blessed through you"

God's promises are always connected to His purpose.

We are not just called from the world; we are called for the glory of God and the blessing of others.

4. OUR CALL TODAY

Like Abraham, we are:

- Called out of the world's system.
- Called to be with God in relationship.
- Called to go with the Gospel.

God's call is not only for the patriarchs of faith—it's for us today. You may not be asked to move geographically, but you are certainly being asked to move spiritually: from self to surrender, from fear to faith, from comfort to calling.

REFLECTION

1. What comfort zone is God asking you to leave?
2. Are you waiting for clarity when God is asking for obedience?
3. How are you actively walking in the promises God has spoken over your life?

PRAYER

Father, thank You for the example of Abraham. Help me to hear Your call and respond with faith, even when the destination is unclear. Give me the courage to leave behind what is familiar and follow You into the unknown. May my life be anchored in Your promises and lived for Your purposes. In Jesus' name. Amen.

73

When You're Not in the Right Place

"Then God said to Jacob, 'Arise, go up to Bethel and dwell there; and make an altar there to God, who appeared to you when you fled from the face of Esau your brother'" (Genesis 35:1, NKJV).

Jacob's story is a reminder that being in the wrong place spiritually—even when it looks comfortable—can carry painful consequences. God met Jacob at Bethel, where Jacob made a vow. But instead of staying where God called him, Jacob settled in Shechem, a place of compromise. This decision had a ripple effect on his entire family.

1. THE COST OF BEING OUT OF PLACE

Though Jacob built an altar in Shechem and tried to honor God, it wasn't where he was supposed to be. The result?

- His daughter was violated.
- His sons committed mass murder.
- His family became vulnerable to retaliation.
- Idolatry crept into his household.

Partial obedience is still disobedience.

Jacob's misplacement opened the door to chaos. It's a warning: When we settle in places God never intended, we forfeit peace and protection.

2. THE INFLUENCE OF OUR ACTIONS

Rachel carried idols with her from her father's house—and her children followed suit. Jacob's failure to lead firmly in worship and obedience led to spiritual compromise in his home.

What parents tolerate, children normalize.

Your walk with God isn't just about you—it affects your entire household.

3. GOD'S GRACE STILL CALLS US BACK

In Jacob's failure, God didn't abandon him. He gave him another chance: "Go back to Bethel." Bethel was the place of encounter, the place of promise, and the place of worship.

God is always calling us back to intimacy, worship, and obedience.

4. RETURNING REQUIRES CLEANSING

Before Jacob could return to Bethel, he called his household to:
- Put away foreign gods.
- Purify themselves.
- Change their garments.

True return to God begins with repentance and cleansing. You can't bring your idols with you into the presence of God.

5. RADICAL OBEDIENCE BRINGS DIVINE PROTECTION

Jacob obeyed, and Scripture says the terror of God fell on the surrounding cities. What should have destroyed them instead backed away. Why? Because God honors radical obedience.

Obedience may feel risky—but disobedience is far more dangerous.

REFLECTION

1. Are you in the place God called you to be—spiritually, emotionally, and physically?
2. Have you compromised by settling in your own "Shechem"?
3. What idols or attitudes do you need to lay down as you return to Bethel?

PRAYER

Father, forgive me for the times I've chosen convenience over obedience. I want to return to the place You've called me—the place of encounter and worship. Cleanse my heart, purify my home, and give me the courage to walk in obedience no matter what the cost. In Jesus' name. Amen.

74

The Key to Successful Daily Living

"For to be carnally minded is death; but to be spiritually minded is life and peace" (Romans 8:6, KJV).

"Walk in the Spirit, and ye shall not fulfil the lust of the flesh" (Galatians 5:16, KJV).

The secret to successful daily living as a believer is not rooted in personal strength, willpower, or even moral discipline—it is found in one life-transforming command: "Walk in the Spirit." The moment we are saved, our inner reality changes. We receive a new heart, a new spirit, and a new Master. Yet, our old flesh and its desires remain. So what determines victory or defeat? The daily decision to walk in the Spirit.

1. WHAT CHANGED WHEN WE BECAME CHRISTIANS

- A new heart – God replaced our deceitful, hardened heart with one responsive to Him (Ezekiel 36:26).
- A new spirit – We became spiritually alive and sensitive to God's voice.
- A new identity – We are new creations in Christ (2 Corinthians 5:17).
- A new Master – We no longer follow the father of lies (John 8:44) but the voice of the Good Shepherd (John 10:27–28).

In Christ, the power of sin is broken—but the presence of sin still battles for control.

2. WHAT DID NOT CHANGE

Our flesh—our old urges and sinful patterns—still exists. The mind must now be renewed daily, and the will must be submitted to the Spirit.

Just because we are saved doesn't mean we are automatically Spirit-led. Daily surrender is required.

3. WALKING IN THE SPIRIT: WHAT IT IS AND ISN'T

- It's not a feeling or an emotional high.
- It's not a license to do whatever feels right.
- It's not legalistic obedience to a set of rules.

Instead, walking in the Spirit is:

- Living in step with God's will and Word.
- Allowing the Holy Spirit to govern your thoughts, desires, and actions.
- A lifestyle of yieldedness, discernment, and trust.

4. WHY IT MATTERS

Romans 8 reminds us that a carnal mind leads to death—spiritual deadness, confusion, anxiety. But a spiritual mind leads to life and peace. In Galatians 5:16, Paul reveals a promise: if we walk in the Spirit, we will not fulfill the lusts of the flesh.

The Spirit leads us into freedom, not bondage (2 Corinthians 3:17). It is by His power that we can overcome sin, fear, and failure.

REFLECTION

1. Are you living each day led by your old desires or by the Holy Spirit?
2. Have you asked the Holy Spirit today to guide your decisions and purify your thoughts?
3. What steps can you take today to align your life more closely with the Spirit's leading?

PRAYER

Holy Spirit, I need You. I confess that I cannot live this life in my own strength. Teach me to walk with You daily. Help me to hear Your voice, to follow Your prompting, and to resist the pull of the flesh. Fill me with Your power and peace so that I may live each day in freedom and victory. In Jesus' name. Amen.

75

Joseph: A Quiet Man of Unshakable Character

"Joseph, to whom she was engaged, was a righteous man and did not want to disgrace her publicly, so he decided to break the engagement quietly" (Matthew 1:19, NLT).

When we think of the birth of Jesus, our focus often turns to Mary—the favored one, the servant of God. Yet beside her stands a man of deep integrity, chosen by God to be the earthly father of the Messiah. Joseph's role, though quiet and often overlooked, speaks volumes about what it means to be a person of character, faith, and courage.

1. JOSEPH'S CHARACTER: RIGHTEOUSNESS IN ACTION

Joseph was engaged to Mary when he discovered she was pregnant. He knew the child wasn't his—and by the law, he had the right to expose her. But rather than react in anger or revenge, he chose compassion.

Righteousness isn't just about keeping rules—it's about how we treat others when we're hurt.

Joseph's decision to divorce her quietly shows a heart that values mercy over judgment. His quiet strength preserved Mary's dignity and positioned him for a divine encounter.

2. JOSEPH'S FAITH: TRUSTING IN THE IMPOSSIBLE

As Joseph considered his next steps, God met him in a dream. The message was startling: "Don't be afraid . . . the child is from the Holy Spirit."

This required radical faith. Joseph had to believe something never heard of before—a virgin carrying the Son of God. And not only believe it, but act on it.

Faith isn't always loud. Sometimes it looks like obedience in the face of uncertainty.

Joseph didn't argue, delay, or seek public validation. He simply obeyed.

3. JOSEPH'S COURAGE: EMBRACING GOD'S PLAN

By taking Mary as his wife and naming the child Jesus, Joseph became the boy's legal father. He stepped into a position of great responsibility and probable social scorn.

Courage isn't the absence of fear—it's moving forward despite it, because God said so.

Joseph's courage protected Mary, preserved the miracle of the virgin birth, and helped fulfill prophecy. His obedience helped usher in the greatest story ever told.

4. THE LEGACY OF A QUIET SERVANT

Joseph never speaks a recorded word in Scripture—but his actions speak louder than words ever could. He teaches us that greatness in God's Kingdom is not found in platform or popularity, but in obedience, humility, and faithfulness.

Sometimes your greatest act of faith is to believe God in silence and follow Him in secret.

REFLECTION

1. Are you willing to obey God even when others misunderstand?
2. Do you respond to hurt with mercy or with judgment?
3. What step of quiet courage is God asking you to take today?

PRAYER

Father, thank You for the example of Joseph—a man of integrity, faith, and courage. Help me to walk in quiet obedience, to value mercy over judgment, and to trust You when the path is unclear. May my life speak of Your faithfulness, even when my words fall short. In Jesus' name. Amen.

The Display of 24-Karat Pure Gold in Your Life

76

Believing God for the Impossible

"And Mary said, Behold the handmaid of the Lord; be it unto me according to thy word" (Luke 1:38, KJV).

"For with God nothing shall be impossible" (Luke 1:37, KJV).

Mary's story is one of wonder, surrender, and deep, enduring faith. She was a young woman from a small town, engaged to a carpenter, and likely envisioning a quiet life. Yet, in a single divine moment, her life was forever changed. God interrupted her plans with His purpose—and she responded with courageous trust.

1. THE CALL CAN COME FROM ANYWHERE

Mary was from Nazareth—a town of no reputation (John 1:46). She was young, unknown, and likely poor. But God delights in using the unlikely to accomplish the impossible.

Your background doesn't disqualify you from God's calling. In fact, it often positions you perfectly for His power to be seen.

2. THE ANNOUNCEMENT OF THE IMPOSSIBLE

The angel didn't bring a simple message—he brought a divine mystery: "You will conceive a child . . . the Son of God."

Mary's immediate response wasn't denial, but honest inquiry: "How can this be?" She didn't lack faith—she simply needed clarity. And the answer was beautiful: "The Holy Spirit will come upon you . . . the power of the Most High will overshadow you."

What seems impossible to man is always possible with God.

God doesn't call us to understand everything—just to trust.

3. THE FAITH TO SAY YES

Mary's final words to the angel reveal the heart of surrendered faith: "Be it unto me according to your word."

She didn't need all the answers. She simply believed the promise and embraced the calling, even though it came with hardship, misunderstanding, and personal cost.

Real faith isn't just believing in God's power—it's yielding to His will.

4. THE DIVINE BURDEN

Mary's faith was not without pain.

- She raised a misunderstood child.
- Joseph passed away.
- Her other children struggled to believe.
- Her community doubted.
- She watched her Son be crucified.

Yet, she did not stop believing.

Faith doesn't prevent pain—it provides the strength to endure it.

5. WHAT MARY TEACHES US

- You don't have to fully understand to truly trust.
- God's greatest works are often born through simple obedience.
- You don't need more faith—you need courage to act on the faith you already have.
- With God, nothing is impossible—not even the dreams He has placed in your heart.

REFLECTION

1. Is there an area where you're asking God, "How can this be?"
2. Are you willing to surrender your plans for His?
3. What step of obedience is God asking you to take in faith today?

PRAYER

Lord, like Mary, I may not fully understand Your ways, but I want to trust You completely. Let it be unto me according to Your word. Fill me with courage to step out in faith, even when it seems impossible. Help me to say yes to You in every season. In Jesus' name. Amen.

77

Living with Honor

"Be devoted to one another in love. Honor one another above yourselves" (Romans 12:10).

In a world that often values self-promotion and personal gain, Scripture calls us to live radically different—to live with honor. To honor someone is to recognize and affirm their God-given worth and treat them accordingly. It is a lifestyle that flows from humility, love, and a deep reverence for God's image in every person.

1. HONOR BEGINS WITH LOVE

Romans 12:10 begins with a simple but profound command: "Be devoted to one another in love." Honor isn't a mechanical act—it grows from genuine affection. The more we love like Christ, the more we will value others above ourselves.

Love fuels honor. Without love, honor becomes empty flattery or obligation.

2. HONOR PREFERS OTHERS

The command to "honor one another above yourselves" challenges our human instinct to prioritize our own needs. In God's Kingdom, greatness is found in preferring others, in listening before speaking, and in serving before being served.

True honor says, "I see the value of who you are, and I choose to treat you accordingly."

3. HONOR IN CONFLICT

Even in the early church, conflict was common (see Acts 15 – the Jerusalem Council). But what stands out is how disagreements were handled:

- Each person spoke without interrupting.
- Leaders, like James, offered resolution with wisdom.
- Unity was pursued over personal agenda.

This is a model for us. Honor doesn't mean we avoid conflict—it means we face it with grace, respect, and a heart to preserve unity.

Conflict handled with honor produces deeper trust and stronger relationships.

4. CREATING A CULTURE OF HONOR

Honor isn't a one-time act—it's a culture. It influences how we:
- Speak to and about others
- Submit to authority
- Encourage the discouraged
- Restore the fallen
- Respond to those we disagree with

A culture of honor reflects the heart of Jesus and becomes a witness to the world.

REFLECTION

1. Do I consistently treat others with honor, even those I disagree with?
2. In what area of my life is God calling me to raise the standard of honor?
3. Am I building a culture of honor in my home, church, and community?

PRAYER

Father, thank You for loving me and honoring me with Your grace. Help me to reflect that same honor toward others. Teach me to love deeply, listen humbly, and walk in a way that lifts others up. Let my words and actions point people to You. In Jesus' name. Amen.

78

When God Writes on the Wall

"Suddenly the fingers of a human hand appeared and wrote on the plaster of the wall, near the lampstand in the royal palace. The king watched the hand as it wrote" (Daniel 5:5).

In Daniel 5, King Belshazzar hosts a lavish, irreverent party. With arrogance and reckless pride, he desecrates the holy vessels of God's temple, praising idols of gold and stone. Suddenly, God interrupts the celebration with divine handwriting on the wall. In that moment, everything changes.

God's message—*Mene, Mene, Tekel, Upharsin*—was a declaration of judgment. It serves as both a warning and a lesson for us today: God always sees. He always judges rightly. And He always responds to pride.

1. POOR JUDGMENT LEADS TO SPIRITUAL BLINDNESS

Belshazzar:

- Forgot the lessons of his grandfather, Nebuchadnezzar, who was humbled by God (Daniel 4:37).
- Allowed alcohol and pleasure to cloud his judgment.
- Treated holy things with contempt.
- Praised false gods instead of honoring the true God.

Forgetting what God has done in others leads us to repeat their mistakes.

When we lose our reverence for God, we lose our ability to discern right from wrong.

2. THE PROBLEM OF PRIDE

Proverbs reminds us that:

- "The LORD detests all the proud of heart" (16:5).
- "Pride comes before destruction" (16:18).

Pride caused Belshazzar to ignore God's warnings. It caused him to elevate himself above God. And in the end, it cost him his kingdom.

Pride says, "I know better."

Humility says, "God, You know best."

3. GOD'S GRAFFITI: A MESSAGE TO EVERY HEART

God's writing wasn't just for Belshazzar—it's a message to all who live without regard for Him:

- *Mene* – God has numbered your days.
- *Tekel* – You have been weighed and found lacking.
- *Peres* – Your kingdom will be divided.

This is a call to examine our hearts:

- How are we treating what God calls holy?
- Are we honoring God with our words, actions, and choices?
- Are we living like our days are numbered?

4. THE REMEDY: HUMILITY AND REPENTANCE

Belshazzar knew the truth but chose to ignore it (Daniel 5:22–23). Unlike Nebuchadnezzar, he refused to humble himself—and judgment came swiftly.

God doesn't take pleasure in judgment. His desire is repentance and restoration. But when pride hardens our hearts, even divine warning can fall on deaf ears.

5. GUARDING AGAINST PRIDE: A LOOK AT PETER'S SPIRAL

Peter's own downfall came through a prideful heart, followed by:

- Prayerlessness
- Presumption
- Paranoia
- Peer Pressure
- Paralysis
- Perjury

Even spiritual leaders must guard their hearts against the subtle rise of pride.

REFLECTION
1. Are you listening to God's warnings or ignoring them?
2. Have you treated sacred things casually or with contempt?
3. What "handwriting" might God be placing on the wall of your life?

PRAYER

Lord, help me to walk in humility, never forgetting who You are and what You've done. Remove pride from my heart. Teach me to honor what is holy and to live with reverence for You. May I always be sensitive to Your warnings and quick to repent. Let my life glorify You in every season. In Jesus' name. Amen.

79

Living a Life of Significance

"The Most High rules in the kingdom of men, and gives it to whomever He chooses" (Daniel 4:17, NKJV).

"There is no other god who can deliver like this" (Daniel 3:29).

In the book of Daniel, two stories stand out that speak directly to the nature of significance and divine order: the fiery furnace of Shadrach, Meshach, and Abednego (Daniel 3), and the humbling of King Nebuchadnezzar (Daniel 4). Together, they declare a profound truth for every believer: the path to true greatness begins in humility. The way up—is down.

1. THE KING'S PROCLAMATION: NO ONE DELIVERS LIKE OUR GOD

When the three Hebrew men refused to bow to Nebuchadnezzar's golden image, they chose faithfulness over fear. God responded with a miraculous deliverance in the furnace—and even the pagan king had to acknowledge: "There is no other God who can deliver like this."

Their significance came not from position, power, or influence—but from unshakable allegiance to God. When we stand firm in our faith, even in the fire, God gets the glory—and we walk in His favor.

2. THE KING'S PERSONAL TESTIMONY: FROM PRIDE TO PRAISE

In Daniel 4, Nebuchadnezzar learns that earthly kingdoms are fragile, and pride is dangerous. Though warned through a dream and Daniel's interpretation, he ignored God's call to repentance.

"Is not this the great Babylon I have built . . . by my mighty power and for the glory of my majesty?" (Daniel 4:30).

In that moment, his kingdom was taken from him. He was driven into the wilderness until he acknowledged: "The Most High rules in the affairs of men."

3. THE WAY UP IS DOWN

Nebuchadnezzar's fall wasn't the end—it was the beginning of his restoration. When he looked up in humility, God lifted him up in power.

True significance starts when we surrender.

The world teaches us to climb to greatness. God teaches us to bow low in reverence.

- Promotion comes from God (Psalm 75:6–7).
- Humble yourselves, and He will lift you up (James 4:10).
- God resists the proud, but gives grace to the humble (1 Peter 5:5).

4. LIVING A LIFE OF SIGNIFICANCE

Significance isn't found in recognition, titles, or applause. It's found in:

- Obedience when it's hard.
- Integrity when no one sees.
- Humility in every victory.
- Dependence on God in every challenge.

God wants to use you to impact people, nations, and generations—but it begins by going down in surrender so He can lift you up in purpose.

REFLECTION

1. Am I building my own kingdom or surrendering to God's?
2. Have I embraced humility as the path to significance?
3. What areas of pride do I need to surrender today?

PRAYER

Lord, remind me daily that You are the One who lifts up and brings low. Keep my heart humble before You. Teach me to serve, to surrender, and to trust Your timing. May my life point to Your greatness, not mine. Use me for Your glory as I walk the path of humility. In Jesus' name. Amen.

80

Who Is Controlling You?

"But Daniel purposed in his heart that he would not defile himself with the portion of the king's meat . . ." (Daniel 1:8, KJV).

"Do not conform to the pattern of this world, but be transformed by the renewing of your mind" (Romans 12:2).

In a world constantly trying to shape our values, choices, and identity, the question, "Who is controlling you?" is both timely and vital. From the story of Daniel and his friends in Babylon, we learn what it means to resist cultural pressure and maintain godly convictions in the face of compromise.

1. THE STRATEGY OF CULTURE: CONFORM AND CONTROL

King Nebuchadnezzar had a clear plan: transform Jewish boys into Babylonian thinkers and loyal servants. His strategy included:
- Changing their language.
- Teaching them new literature.
- Giving them new names.
- Offering them new food.

The goal? Erase their identity and values—and replace them with Babylonian ideals.

The enemy still works the same way. He seeks to rename, reeducate, and reshape us to fit the world's mold.

2. THE POWER OF CONVICTION

Daniel drew a line. He "purposed in his heart" not to defile himself. His convictions were not temporary opinions—they were rooted in truth and nurtured from a young age.

Biblical conviction involves:

- A commitment to Scripture as ultimate authority.
- The construction of beliefs based on that truth.
- The courage to live them out, even under pressure.

Convictions give you the courage to say no to compromise and yes to God.

3. CONTROL VS. CONVICTION

A controlling spirit tries to:

- Assume unauthorized authority.
- Blame others while refusing accountability.
- Manipulate through silence, intimidation, or false humility.
- Divide through isolation and behind-the-scenes influence.

These tactics mirror the spirit of Jezebel—designed to weaken, manipulate, and destroy.

But God calls His people to be led by the Holy Spirit, not by fear or domination.

4. DEATH IN THE POT: DISCERN WHAT YOU'RE CONSUMING

Just as Elisha's prophets unknowingly added poison to their stew (2 Kings 4:38–41), we too must be discerning. Not every idea, trend, or teaching is spiritually nutritious.

What we consume—through media, relationships, teaching—can nourish or corrupt us.

Stay rooted in the truth of God's Word. Only His Word brings clarity, life, and spiritual safety.

5. TAKE A STAND IN THE SPIRIT

Jude 1:17–23 urges believers to remain steadfast, build up their faith, pray in the Spirit, and extend mercy with discernment.

We're called to:

- Guard against scoffers and ungodly desires.
- Keep ourselves in God's love.

- Rescue others with truth and compassion.
- Hate what corrupts the soul, while showing mercy to the person.

We stand, not with pride, but with humble dependence on the Holy Spirit.

REFLECTION

1. What are the voices or forces trying to control or influence your decisions?
2. Are you living by convictions or conforming under pressure?
3. What areas of your life need realignment with the Word of God?

PRAYER

Lord, give me a heart like Daniel—bold in conviction and anchored in Your Word. Help me discern the influences in my life and walk by the Spirit, not by fear or cultural pressure. I choose to live surrendered to You, resisting every attempt to steal my God-given identity. In Jesus' name. Amen.

81

You Have What You Tolerate

"When you walk through the fire, you will not be burned; the flames will not set you ablaze" (Isaiah 43:2).

"You shall have no other gods before Me" (Exodus 20:3, NKJV).

We often look at the circumstances of our lives—disorder, compromise, or stagnation—and wonder how things ended up this way. But Scripture teaches us a hard truth: what we tolerate, we eventually live with. Tolerance is not always peacekeeping—it can be quiet permission for bondage to remain.

1. THE POWER OF TOLERANCE

The life you are living today is largely the product of what you have tolerated over the years—whether it's unhealthy thoughts, damaging relationships, sin patterns, or spiritual laziness. God calls us to holy intolerance—a refusal to accept anything less than His will.

If you tolerate fear, it will rule you.

If you tolerate compromise, it will define you.

If you tolerate mediocrity, it will diminish your purpose.

2. LIVING UNDER PRESSURE VS. LIVING BY PRINCIPLE

Shadrach, Meshach, and Abednego were tested in the furnace of peer and fear pressure. The demand was clear: Bow or burn. But they stood firm, not out of defiance—but out of devotion.

Conviction kept them standing when fear pressured them to fall.

They didn't negotiate their worship. They didn't rationalize bowing as survival. They were governed by the principle that God alone is worthy of worship.

3. CONVICTION OVER COMPROMISE
- "Our God" – They knew Him personally.
- "Whom we serve" – Their lives were in submission to Him.
- "He is able" – Their faith was in God's power.
- "But if not . . ." – Their trust was in His sovereignty.

Faith that only trusts when God performs is not faith—it's a transaction.

True faith says, "Even if He doesn't, I will still serve Him."

4. FREEDOM IN THE FIRE

God didn't keep them from the fire—He met them in it. Not a hair was singed, but their bondages were burned off. The fire that was meant to destroy them became the fire that freed them.

There is blessing in the fire when we walk with God.

There is fellowship in the fire when we trust His presence.

God doesn't always deliver us from the fire, but He promises to walk with us through it.

REFLECTION
1. What ungodly attitudes or situations have you tolerated for too long?
2. Are you bowing under the pressure of culture or standing on the truth of God's Word?
3. How can you begin to replace compromise with conviction?

PRAYER

Lord, open my eyes to what I have tolerated that dishonors You. Give me the courage to stand with conviction, even when the pressure is great. Burn off every chain in the fires I face and draw me closer to You. May my life reflect the kind of faith that says, "Even if not, I will still serve You." In Jesus' name. Amen.

82

The Power of Resurrection Faith

"Then went in also that other disciple . . . and he saw and believed" (John 20:8, KJV).

On the first day of the week, while it was still dark, Mary Magdalene visited the tomb—and found the stone rolled away. She ran to Peter and John in alarm, unsure of what had happened. What followed was a powerful moment that would change their lives forever: they saw . . . and they believed.

This simple but profound phrase speaks to the heart of the Christian faith. Faith isn't built on myths or assumptions. It's anchored in the evidence of a risen Savior.

1. THE POWER OF THE EMPTY TOMB

The linen grave clothes were lying there. The napkin was folded neatly by itself. There were no signs of a hurried theft, no struggle, and certainly no body. John saw the emptiness and understood the fullness of its meaning: Jesus was alive.

The empty tomb isn't just proof of a miracle—it's the foundation of our hope.

2. WHAT DID JOHN BELIEVE?

- That Jesus had truly risen—not stolen, not resuscitated.
- That death had been defeated.
- That the words of Jesus were true.

Though they didn't fully understand the Scriptures yet, something supernatural happened in John's heart: he believed.

3. WHY DOES IT MATTER THAT JESUS IS ALIVE?

Romans 4:24–25 tells us:
- He was delivered up for our trespasses.
- He was raised for our justification.

Because Jesus is alive:
- Sin no longer has power over us.
- God has accepted the sacrifice made on our behalf.
- We are declared righteous through faith.

This is not merely intellectual agreement. Romans 10:9–10 reminds us that salvation comes by believing in the heart and confessing with the mouth.

4. THE CALL TO BELIEVE

John 20:31 gives the reason the Gospel was written:

"That ye might believe that Jesus is the Christ, the Son of God; and that believing ye might have life through his name" (KJV).

Faith is not seeing everything—it's seeing enough to trust God with what we don't yet understand.

If you've been questioning, doubting, or living in fear—come again to the empty tomb. Look. See. And believe.

REFLECTION

1. What does resurrection mean to you personally?
2. Have you truly believed—not just intellectually, but with your whole heart?
3. What is God calling you to trust Him with today, even if you can't see the full picture?

PRAYER

Risen Lord, thank You for the cross and for the empty tomb. Help me to see with eyes of faith. Strengthen my belief that You are alive and victorious. Let the power of Your resurrection transform how I live today—in freedom, in hope, and in confidence. In Jesus' name. Amen.

83

When the Strong Feel Weak

"Elijah was a man with a nature like ours . . ." (James 5:17, ESV).

"He came to a broom bush, sat down under it and prayed that he might die. 'I have had enough, LORD,' he said" (1 Kings 19:4).

Even the strongest among us can feel broken. Elijah—prophet, miracle-worker, and fearless voice of God—found himself under a tree, exhausted, isolated, and ready to give up. After calling down fire from heaven and standing alone against false prophets, this mighty man of God wanted to die.

His story reminds us of a powerful truth: spiritual people still battle emotional pain. Elijah's depression wasn't a failure of faith—it was a cry of exhaustion from a deeply human soul.

1. EVEN HEROES BREAK DOWN

James 5:17 tells us that Elijah was "a man just like us." That's not a dismissal—it's a reminder. Even those who walk closely with God can wrestle with depression, discouragement, and deep weariness.

Victory on the mountain doesn't mean we're immune to valleys.

Sometimes, the greatest attacks come right after our greatest wins.

2. ELIJAH'S DOWNWARD SPIRAL

Elijah's journey into despair came through a series of missteps:
- He focused on fear instead of faith (1 Kings 19:3).
- He isolated himself from companionship.
- He allowed exhaustion to deplete his strength.

- He fell into self-pity, believing he was alone and defeated.

We see his emotional spiral—overwhelmed, undernourished, and overstimulated by pressure. His cry, "I am no better than my fathers," shows how pain distorts perspective.

3. GOD'S COMPASSIONATE RESPONSE

God didn't rebuke Elijah. He met him in his weakness with:
- Rest – "The journey is too much for you" (1 Kings 19:7).
- Provision – Food and water for his body.
- Presence – A whisper, not a wind. Not fire. Just God's nearness.
- Purpose – A renewed assignment and a reminder that Elijah was not alone.

God's healing often begins with rest, is followed by nourishment, and is fulfilled in a renewed calling.

4. WE NEED EACH OTHER

Elijah left his servant behind. But healing came, in part, when God gave him Elisha, a faithful companion to walk alongside him. One of the enemy's greatest weapons is isolation. One of God's greatest gifts is community.

Don't battle in silence. God often sends healing through relationship.

REFLECTION

1. Are you carrying a weight of despair or emotional exhaustion today?
2. Have you isolated yourself like Elijah?
3. Are you listening for God's whisper in the stillness?

PRAYER

Father, thank You for understanding the burdens I carry, even when I don't have the words to explain them. When I feel overwhelmed, remind me that You are near. Help me find rest in You, strength in Your Word, and comfort in godly companionship. Teach me to listen for Your whisper, and give me the courage to keep going. In Jesus' name. Amen.

84

A Journey of Surrender and Succession

"So Elisha returned to his oxen and slaughtered them... Then he went with Elijah as his assistant" (1 Kings 19:21, NLT).

"When the LORD was about to take Elijah up to heaven in a whirlwind, Elijah and Elisha were on their way from Gilgal" (2 Kings 2:1).

The passing of the mantle from Elijah to Elisha is one of the most profound transitions in all of Scripture. It reveals the heart of mentorship, the cost of following God's call, and the path of spiritual succession. This journey wasn't just about power—it was about process, preparation, and personal surrender.

1. ELISHA BURNED HIS PLOW – NO TURNING BACK

When Elisha received Elijah's initial call, he didn't hesitate. He burned his plow and sacrificed his oxen—symbolically severing ties to his past life. It was a bold, permanent decision that said, "I'm all in."

To receive God's future, you must fully release your past.

Radical obedience often requires radical separation.

2. THE JOURNEY OF TRANSITION: GILGAL TO JORDAN

Elijah's final journey before his departure took him and Elisha through four symbolic locations, each marking a stage in spiritual maturity:

- **Gilgal – The Place of Beginnings.** Where Israel first camped in the Promised Land. It's where your journey starts, but not where you stay. God calls you to movement, not maintenance.

- **Bethel – The Place of Prayer.** "House of God." A place of communion and altar-building. Before God uses you in power, He forms you in intimacy.
- **Jericho – The Place of Battle.** The site of one of Israel's greatest victories. Your calling will be tested. Battles are part of your building.
- **Jordan – The Place of Death.** Not just physical death, but death to self. Elijah crossed and was taken. Elisha crossed and received the mantle. Before the mantle is passed, the self must die.

3. THE MANTLE IS RECEIVED, NOT TAKEN

Elisha didn't demand the mantle. He followed faithfully, served humbly, and asked boldly: "Let me inherit a double portion of your spirit."

The anointing flows through servanthood, not ambition.

4. THE COST OF DOUBLE PORTION

Elisha's journey wasn't glamorous. He washed Elijah's hands (2 Kings 3:11), endured tests, and resisted distractions. But his persistence prepared him for greater responsibility.

God prepares in secret before He promotes in public.

5. LEAVING A LEGACY

Elijah's legacy didn't end with his departure and lived on through Elisha, who did even greater miracles. When we invest in others and pour into the next generation, our impact multiplies.

A true leader isn't just successful, they're successional.

REFLECTION

1. What part of your past do you need to "burn" to fully follow God's call?
2. Are you embracing the process, or rushing for the mantle?
3. Who are you following? Who are you pouring into?

PRAYER

Father, help me to walk the journey from Gilgal to Jordan with faith and surrender. Teach me to serve faithfully, pray earnestly, and die daily to self. Prepare me to receive all that You have for me—and to pass it on with honor and humility. In Jesus' name. Amen.

85

Claiming the Promises

"The LORD is trustworthy in all he promises and faithful in all he does" (Psalm 145:13).

The promises of God are not passive guarantees—they are invitations to active faith. In 1 Kings 18, Elijah receives a clear word from God: "I will send rain." Yet what follows is not Elijah waiting idly but engaging deeply in prayer. Why? Because God's promises must often be birthed through persistent prayer and obedient action.

1. EVERY PROMISE HAS A PROCESS

God promised rain—but only after Elijah presented himself to Ahab (1 Kings 18:1). The promise was personal and conditional. God's movement often requires our movement.

When God wants to bless you, He may use a person.

When God speaks a promise, He also invites your obedience.

2. FAITH SPEAKS BEFORE THE STORM

Elijah boldly declares, "There is the sound of a heavy rain" (1 Kings 18:41), even when the sky was completely clear. His faith wasn't based on the forecast—but on God's word.

Faith declares what it hears from heaven, not what it sees on earth.

3. BIRTHING THE PROMISE THROUGH PRAYER

Elijah didn't assume that the promise would fulfill itself. He climbed Mount Carmel, bent down, and interceded persistently—seven times—until he saw the first sign: a cloud the size of a man's hand (1 Kings 18:42–44).

God's promises are not magic—they are a partnership.

Prayer is the womb where the promise is formed and brought to life.

4. THE POSTURE OF EFFECTIVE PRAYER

Elijah's approach gives us a model for powerful, effective prayer:

- Separation – He went up alone to seek God (Matthew 6:6).
- Humility – He bowed low, his face between his knees (1 Peter 5:6).
- Specificity – He gave clear instruction to look toward the sea.
- Persistence – He didn't stop after one attempt—he sent his servant seven times.
- Expectancy – He anticipated the breakthrough even when all he saw was a small cloud.

Don't just pray—pray like you expect the rain.

5. AFTER THE FIRE, COMES THE BATTLE

Elijah had just called down fire from heaven in a single prayer. But bringing the rain took longer. Sometimes, the next promise requires deeper wrestling, even after great victories.

Don't let previous breakthroughs cause you to underestimate the persistence required for the next one.

REFLECTION

1. What has God promised you that still feels delayed?
2. Are you partnering with Him through obedience and intercession?
3. Do your prayers reflect faith, humility, and expectancy?

PRAYER

Faithful Father, thank You for Your trustworthy promises. Teach me to partner with You—not just to receive, but to pray, obey, and believe. Like Elijah, help me press in, even when I see nothing. Strengthen me to persevere until the cloud appears, until the breakthrough comes, until the rain falls. In Jesus' name. Amen.

86

The Power of Grace Over Judgment

"Let him who is without sin among you be the first to throw a stone at her" (John 8:7, ESV).

In one of the most profound moments of Jesus' ministry, a woman caught in the act of adultery is brought before Him. Her accusers demand justice, quoting Moses' law. But Jesus, in wisdom and grace, rewrites the narrative—not by denying sin, but by redefining how we respond to it.

This story reminds us of a central truth of the Gospel: God's grace doesn't excuse sin—but it rescues sinners.

1. THE WOMAN IN THE STORY – A MIRROR FOR US ALL

We don't know her name, but we know her guilt. Caught in the act, dragged into public shame, and used as a pawn to trap Jesus, she stood condemned by the law.

But James 2:10 reminds us that whoever breaks even one part of the law is guilty of all.

Before we lift a stone at someone else's sin, Scripture humbles us: We are all in need of mercy.

2. THE ACCUSERS – RELIGIOUS BUT NOT RIGHTEOUS

The scribes and Pharisees knew the law, but they didn't know the heart of God. Their motives were clear:
- They used the woman, not to save her, but to trap Jesus.
- They could condemn, but not restore.
- They were religious, but not righteous.

"It is a terrible thing for a sinner to fall into the hands of his fellow sinner" (F.B. Meyer).

Religious pride can blind us to our own brokenness. It whispers, "At least I'm better than them." But true holiness always walks hand in hand with humility.

3. THE RESPONSE OF JESUS – GRACE AND TRUTH

Jesus neither condoned the woman's sin nor condemned her. He silenced her accusers with one challenge: "He who is without sin . . . let him cast the first stone."

And one by one, stones fell from the hands of the self-righteous.

Jesus didn't ignore the sin—but He offered something better than judgment: grace.

He said to the woman: "Neither do I condemn you. Go, and sin no more."

This is the Gospel: Not condemnation, but invitation. An invitation to leave sin behind, because we've been loved and forgiven.

4. THE ENCOUNTER THAT CHANGES EVERYTHING

The woman came expecting judgment. She left transformed by mercy. What law couldn't do—restore her—grace did.

One moment in the presence of Jesus can rewrite your story.

REFLECTION

1. Are you quick to pick up stones or slow to show grace?
2. Is there someone you've judged that God is calling you to forgive?
3. How has Jesus responded to you in your lowest moments?

PRAYER

Lord, help me to see others through Your eyes. Teach me to lay down my stones of judgment and pick up the tools of mercy. Let me never forget that I, too, have been forgiven much. May I walk in grace, speak with compassion, and love like You. In Jesus' name. Amen.

87

When God Says "Enough"

"My Spirit shall not strive with man forever" (Genesis 6:3, NKJV).

"They will be destroyed suddenly, broken in an instant beyond all hope of healing" (Proverbs 6:15, NLT).

God is merciful. He is long-suffering, patient, and compassionate beyond our understanding. Yet Scripture is clear: there is a point when God says, "Enough." When persistent rebellion, unrepentant hearts, and willful wickedness defy Him for too long, His mercy gives way to judgment.

This isn't because God delights in punishing people—it's because He is just, and justice demands that sin be addressed.

1. GOD'S PATIENCE IS NOT PERMISSION

Proverbs 6 describes people who lie, stir up trouble, and plot evil. Though they may seem to get away with their wickedness, verse 15 declares a sobering reality: "They will be destroyed suddenly... beyond all hope of healing."

Ahab and Jezebel learned this firsthand (1 Kings 21). Their abuse of power, idolatry, and injustice against Naboth led God to speak judgment through Elijah. Though God waited, gave chances, and sent warnings, they pushed beyond the limit.

God's patience has a purpose—to lead us to repentance, not to give us time to harden our hearts.

2. HISTORICAL EXAMPLES OF GOD'S SEVERITY

Throughout Scripture, we see moments when God's mercy ended and His judgment came:

- Sodom and Gomorrah – immorality and pride led to total destruction.
- Herod Agrippa – glorifying himself rather than God resulted in his sudden death (Acts 12:21–23).
- Judah – repeated rejection of prophets led to Babylonian exile (2 Chronicles 36:11–16).
- Ahab and Jezebel – injustice, idolatry, and bloodshed led to a dramatic downfall (1 Kings 21).

These aren't just stories—they are warnings and reminders of the holiness of God.

3. AHAB: A CASE STUDY IN GOD'S FINAL WORD

Ahab was deeply influenced by Jezebel and gave himself fully to evil. God's message to him was sharp:

"You have sold yourself to do what is evil . . . I will bring disaster on you . . ." (1 Kings 21:20–21).

He chose to ignore God, and judgment came—not because God was cruel, but because God is holy and His patience had been exhausted.

4. GOD'S WORD STANDS – NO ONE CAN STOP IT

There is an end to God's patience. No one knows it. God keeps His word. No one stops it.

This is not a message of fear—but a call to sober reflection. God's mercy is available right now, but we must not take it for granted. Every call to repentance is an opportunity to return before the line is crossed.

REFLECTION

1. Am I ignoring any clear convictions or warnings from God?
2. Have I mistaken God's patience for approval?
3. Is there any area in my life where I need to say, "Enough" before God does?

PRAYER

Lord, thank You for Your mercy and patience. Forgive me for the times I have delayed obedience or ignored Your voice. Help me to walk in reverence and humility, knowing that You are both merciful and just. Soften my heart, correct my path, and keep me aligned with Your will. In Jesus' name. Amen.

88

Where Is Your Treasure?

"For where your treasure is, there will your heart be also" (Matthew 6:21, KJV).

We all treasure something. Whether it's success, security, possessions, or people—our hearts naturally follow our investments. Jesus' teaching in Matthew 6:19–24 isn't a prohibition against wealth, but a redirection of our priorities toward what truly lasts: eternity.

1. TWO TREASURES: EARTHLY AND HEAVENLY

Jesus invites us to compare two types of treasures:
- Earthly treasure is temporary. It can rust, rot, or be stolen.
- Heavenly treasure is eternal. It never fades and is forever secure.

You are not discouraged from storing treasure—you are simply instructed where to store it.

Every decision to give, serve, or surrender is a deposit in heaven's account.

2. TREASURE AND THE HEART

Jesus makes a striking connection: "Where your treasure is, there will your heart be also."

In other words, your heart follows your investments. If your treasure is in possessions, your heart will be anchored to the temporary. But if your treasure is in God's Kingdom, your heart will be aligned with His purposes.

Show me your spending and your schedule, and I can often tell you your true treasure.

3. THE LIGHT OF YOUR EYE

Jesus continues: "If your eye is single (clear, focused), your whole body will be full of light . . ." (Matthew 6:22).

This speaks to focus and clarity. A heart focused on Kingdom stewardship is like a bright light—it brings direction and purpose. But divided loyalty clouds our vision and leads to darkness.

A generous eye brings clarity. A greedy eye brings confusion.

4. TWO MASTERS: GOD OR MAMMON

You cannot serve both God and money. One will have your devotion; the other will always take second place.

Serving God means holding everything else with open hands:
- Your finances
- Your plans
- Your possessions
- Your time

As Martin Luther once said, "Whatever I have placed in God's hands, that I still possess."

5. THE OPEN HAND PRINCIPLE

God blesses hands that are open—not clinging but trusting. Corrie Ten Boom once remarked, "I have learned to hold all things loosely, so God will not have to pry them out of my hands."

Stewardship is about trust—believing that what we release into God's hands is never lost, but transformed into something eternal.

REFLECTION

1. Where is your treasure right now—and where is your heart?
2. Are you serving God with an open hand or clinging to temporary things?
3. What would it look like for you to invest in the Kingdom today?

PRAYER

Lord, help me to treasure what truly matters. Teach me to give freely, live faithfully, and invest in Your eternal Kingdom. Open my eyes to see the value of heavenly treasure, and give me the courage to surrender what I cannot keep, to gain what I cannot lose. In Jesus' name. Amen.

89

Faith, Obedience, and Generational Continuity

"The oil stopped flowing" (2 Kings 4:6).

This story from 2 Kings 4:1–7 is more than just a miracle account; it is a profound lesson in faith, stewardship, and the importance of obedience across generations. A widow facing desperate circumstances reaches out to the prophet Elisha—and what begins as a crisis ends in a miraculous overflow. But the oil only flowed as long as obedience and expectation remained alive.

1. A DESPERATE CRY AND A DIVINE QUESTION

The widow's situation was dire: her husband had died, her sons were about to be sold, and all she had was a small flask of oil. Elisha's question wasn't just practical—it was prophetic: "What do you have in the house?"

God always begins with what you already have.

You may think it's small, but in God's hands, small things become miraculous sources.

2. YOUR OBEDIENCE CREATES SPACE FOR THE MIRACLE

Elisha's instructions were simple but specific:
- Borrow empty jars.
- Go inside.
- Shut the door.
- Pour the oil.

The miracle didn't happen instantly. It happened as she poured—as she obeyed.

Obedience opened the door for overflow.

The oil didn't come from nowhere—it flowed from the little she had, and God multiplied it as she acted in faith.

3. THE INVOLVEMENT OF THE NEXT GENERATION

The sons weren't bystanders—they were part of the process.

They fetched jars, helped close the door, and responded to their mother's request: "Bring me another jar."

But the response that followed was pivotal: "There aren't any more." And the oil stopped.

The miracle was not limited by God, but by capacity.

When there was no more expectation, no more empty vessels, the flow ceased.

4. KEEP THE OIL FLOWING

This is a message to us today: The oil—the anointing, provision, and presence of God—keeps flowing when faith keeps acting.

When we run out of hunger, preparation, or obedience, the oil stops.

Every generation must participate to keep the move of God going. The next generation must:

- Be willing to carry the jars.
- Be taught the value of obedience.
- Be positioned to expect more.

REFLECTION

1. What "oil" has God given you to steward?
2. Are you preparing space for God to move, or have you limited the flow?
3. How are you including the next generation in what God is doing in your life?

PRAYER

Lord, thank You for the oil—for Your Spirit, Your provision, and Your faithfulness. Help me to keep preparing, keep pouring, and keep believing. Teach me to involve others—especially the next generation—so that Your miracles may continue. May I never run out of expectation or obedience. In Jesus' name. Amen.

90

Sowing into God's Future

"Do not be deceived: God is not mocked, for whatever one sows, that will he also reap" (Galatians 6:7, ESV).

Life is not random. In God's economy, everything operates by spiritual laws—and one of the most powerful is the Law of the Seed. According to this principle, everything you sow—whether good or evil, physical or spiritual, will eventually produce a harvest.

1. THE SEED REPRESENTS A BEGINNING

A seed may appear small and insignificant, but within it lies potential, purpose, and power.

- It's the beginning of something bigger.
- It's a bridge to your future.
- It is proof of your faith and expectation.

When you plant a seed—whether it's an act of love, generosity, obedience, or sacrifice—you send an instruction to your future.

"As long as the earth endures, seedtime and harvest . . . will never cease" (Genesis 8:22).

2. YOU REAP WHAT YOU SOW

The Bible is clear: your results are directly connected to your actions.

- Sow righteousness → reap reward (Proverbs 11:18).
- Sow iniquity → reap trouble (Proverbs 22:8).
- Dig a pit for others → fall into it yourself (Proverbs 26:27).

Even David, a man after God's heart, experienced the law of the seed through both mercy and consequence (2 Samuel 12). What we sow, we will eventually face.

You cannot sow dishonor and reap blessing. You cannot sow apathy and reap anointing.

3. YOU REAP IN A DIFFERENT SEASON

Seeds don't grow overnight.

- "In due time" – God operates in seasons, not seconds.
- Hannah waited for her child (1 Samuel 1:20).
- Farmers wait for the rain.
- And we too must learn to trust the process.

"Let us not grow weary in doing good, for in due season we will reap, if we do not give up" (Galatians 6:9).

Waiting is not a sign of failure—it's the incubation of your harvest.

4. YOU REAP IN PROPORTION TO WHAT YOU SOW

- Sow little → reap little.
- Sow generously → reap generously (2 Corinthians 9:6).
- Your level of investment determines your level of return.

Jesus taught this too: "With the measure you use, it will be measured to you" (Luke 6:38).

What kind of harvest do you want? The answer determines how you sow today.

REFLECTION

1. What are you sowing into your life, family, and future right now?
2. Are you sowing in the Spirit or in the flesh?
3. Are you trusting God for the "due season" or growing weary in the wait?

PRAYER

Lord, thank You for the divine law of the seed. Help me to be intentional with what I sow—my words, my time, my finances, and my relationships. Give me the faith to plant in hope and the endurance to wait for the harvest. Teach me to sow into the Spirit so that I may reap life everlasting. In Jesus' name. Amen.

91

When Jesus Touches the Untouchable

"When Jesus came down from the mountainside, large crowds followed him. A man with leprosy came and knelt before him and said, 'Lord, if you are willing, you can make me clean'" (Matthew 8:1–2).

In a moment packed with power and tenderness, a man marked by disease and social rejection broke through the crowd to encounter Jesus. Though many followed Christ that day, it was the least likely person—a leper—who truly worshipped Him.

1. HE WAS THE LEAST—YET HE WORSHIPPED

Leprosy made this man an outcast, forced to live outside the community, untouched and unseen. And yet, he came. He pressed through shame, rejection, and religious barriers not just to ask—but to worship.

Worship is most powerful when it comes from a broken, desperate heart. The leper shows us that even the unworthy can worship when they truly see who Jesus is.

2. HE WORSHIPPED BEFORE HE ASKED

The leper knelt before Jesus—not as a beggar, but as a believer. Before he asked for healing, he gave honor. His posture was worshipful, not transactional. True worship isn't about what we want—it's about who He is.

3. HE BELIEVED IN BOTH THE POWER AND THE HEART OF JESUS

He said, "Lord, if you are willing . . ."— not doubting Christ's ability, but submitting to His heart. He trusted Jesus to be both able and willing.

Faith doesn't demand. It trusts the heart of the Healer even when the answer is slow or different than expected.

4. JESUS TOUCHED WHAT OTHERS WOULDN'T

In that moment, Jesus did what was unthinkable: He touched the man. He didn't have to. He could have spoken a word. But Jesus reached beyond the rules to affirm dignity and restore identity. The touch of Jesus didn't make Jesus unclean—it made the leper whole.

5. CAN JESUS TOUCH THE HIDDEN, SHAMEFUL PARTS OF YOU?

We all carry "leprous" places—wounds, secrets, sins, shame—that we try to keep hidden. But Jesus isn't afraid of our mess. He is still willing. He is still able. And He still touches what others avoid.

Let Him into the parts of your life you've kept hidden.

Worship opens the door. His touch brings the healing.

REFLECTION

1. What area of your life do you feel too ashamed to bring to Jesus?
2. Are you worshipping only when you have a request, or are you honoring Him first?
3. Do you believe He is willing—not just able—to meet your need?

PRAYER

Lord, thank You for being the God who touches the untouchable and heals the broken. Today, I bring You my hidden places—the parts I've been ashamed of. I worship You not only for what You can do, but for who You are. Touch me, cleanse me, and make me whole again. In Jesus' name. Amen.

92

Unlocking the Power of Unity

"Again I say unto you, That if two of you shall agree on earth as touching any thing that they shall ask, it shall be done for them of my Father which is in heaven" (Matthew 18:19, KJV).

There is a spiritual law woven into the fabric of creation that holds remarkable power: the Law of Agreement. When two people come together in harmony—sharing one heart, one purpose, and one prayer—heaven responds.

1. WHAT IS AGREEMENT?

Agreement is more than simply saying "yes." It's harmony in spirit, unity in action, and alignment in purpose. Like a symphony where each instrument plays its part, agreement creates spiritual resonance that attracts heaven's attention.

Agreement is a sound heaven cannot ignore.

Where there is true unity, there is divine authority.

2. THE EXPONENTIAL POWER OF AGREEMENT

Scripture shows us the multiplying power of unity:

- "How should one chase a thousand, and two put ten thousand to flight . . ." (Deuteronomy 32:30).
- "Two are better than one . . . for if they fall, one will lift the other" (Ecclesiastes 4:9–11).

When we stand in agreement—with each other and with God—we activate supernatural power. Battles are won, burdens are lifted, and miracles are released.

Unity multiplies what individual strength alone could never accomplish.

3. HEAVEN OPERATES ON AGREEMENT

The nature of God Himself—Father, Son, and Holy Spirit—is rooted in perfect unity. Heaven is a place of agreement, order, and alignment. When Satan introduced discord in heaven, he was cast down. When Adam and Eve stepped out of alignment with God, brokenness entered the world.

Where there is disagreement, there is powerlessness.

Where there is agreement, there is peace, purpose, and power.

4. THE POWER OF TWO

Jesus didn't say, "If a multitude agrees." He said, "If two agree . . ." That means you and one other person—united in prayer and faith—can move the heart of God.

- Two to come together.
- Two to pray.
- Two to believe.

Heaven doesn't need numbers; it responds to unity.

5. A WARNING FROM NAZARETH

In Matthew 13:58, Jesus could do few miracles in His hometown—not because He lacked power, but because there was no agreement, no faith. Their familiarity bred unbelief. Their disagreement shut down the miraculous.

Agreement creates a channel for God's power.

Disagreement builds a wall against it.

REFLECTION

1. Who are you walking in agreement with—your spouse, friends, church, or coworkers?
2. Are your relationships marked by unity or strife?
3. Are you agreeing with God's promises over your life—or doubting them?

PRAYER

Father, thank You for the power of agreement. Teach me to walk in unity—with You and with others. Help me guard my heart from division, offense, and isolation. May my relationships reflect the harmony of heaven, and may my prayers carry the power of unified faith. In Jesus' name. Amen.

93

Growth Is a Kingdom Principle

"And God blessed them, and God said unto them, Be fruitful, and multiply . . ." (Genesis 1:28, KJV).

From the very beginning, God embedded into creation the principle of increase. In Eden, God's command to Adam and Eve was not merely survival—it was fruitfulness, multiplication, and dominion. This reveals God's heart: He delights in growth. He calls us not just to maintain but to multiply.

1. INCREASE IS A DIVINE EXPECTATION

You're either increasing or decreasing—there's no neutral ground. Jesus taught this through the Parable of the Talents (Matthew 25:14–30). Each servant was entrusted with resources and expected to steward them with increase.

God gives us ability, but He expects accountability.

Stagnation isn't safety—it's disobedience.

2. INCREASE IN EVERY AREA

God desires increase not only in material areas but in our:

- Faith – "Lord, increase our faith" (Luke 17:5).
- Grace – "Where sin abounded, grace did much more abound" (Romans 5:20).
- Character and Calling – "Let your progress be evident to all" (1 Timothy 4:15).

Growth is not optional—it's spiritual obedience.

3. GROWTH REQUIRES DEVELOPMENT

We are God's workmanship, created for good works (Ephesians 2:10). But even gifts must be sharpened:
- Ability must be trained (Psalm 144:1).
- Skill must be applied (Exodus 35:10).

Like seeds, talents grow only when planted and nurtured.

4. DILIGENCE UNLOCKS INCREASE

Colossians 3:23 reminds us to work heartily, as unto the Lord. The Kingdom of God does not reward laziness—it celebrates excellence.

A heart of honor and hands of diligence attract increase.

Be faithful in the unseen, committed in the routine, and excellent in every task. God sees. God rewards.

5. HONOR IS THE FOUNDATION OF FRUITFULNESS

We must honor:
- What God has given us.
- Who gave it to us.

Malachi 2:2 warns that dishonor closes the door to blessing. Honor unlocks inheritance.

6. RISK IS PART OF INCREASE

Growth requires faith and courage:
- Stepping out when others shrink back.
- Investing even when the outcome is uncertain.
- Trusting that God honors obedience over comfort.

Faith is spelled R-I-S-K. Increase requires trust in the God who multiplies.

REFLECTION

1. Where in your life have you settled for maintenance instead of multiplication?
2. Are you honoring what God has placed in your hands?
3. What one area can you intentionally grow this week—in faith, excellence, or service?

PRAYER

Father, thank You for calling me to increase. I confess that too often I've settled for comfort over growth. Teach me to steward what You've given me with diligence, faith, and honor. Help me multiply—not for my glory, but for Yours. May my life be a testimony of Kingdom increase. In Jesus' name. Amen.

94

Speak Life, Shape Destiny

"Death and life are in the power of the tongue, and they who indulge in it shall eat the fruit of it [for death or life]" (Proverbs 18:21, AMPC).

Words are never empty. According to God's Word, every syllable we speak has the power to build or break, heal or hurt, bless or curse. This is the spiritual law of the power of words: Your life is moving in the direction of your words.

1. EVERYTHING BEGINS WITH A WORD

Creation itself began with spoken words:
"And God said . . ."—again and again in Genesis 1. Light, land, life—all came into being through God's voice.

In the same way, your words give form to your reality. What you declare over your life, your family, your future, and even your pain becomes the framework of your experience.

A thought cannot become reality until it is spoken.

2. YOUR WORDS ARE CREATIVE TOOLS

Jesus said in Matthew 12 that our mouths speak what overflows from our hearts (v. 34), and that we will give account for every careless word (v. 36). Why? Because words create consequences. They are not neutral—they are seeds that bear fruit.

- Speak peace – reap peace.
- Speak fear – reap anxiety.
- Speak truth – build trust.
- Speak defeat – attract despair.

Your present life reflects the words you repeatedly speak to yourself.

3. YOU CAN SHIFT SEASONS WITH YOUR SPEECH

In Mark 5, the woman with the issue of blood "kept saying to herself, 'If I can just touch His garment, I'll be healed.'" Her healing was activated not only by her touch but by her words.

What you say to yourself in faith can move the hand of God.

In the same way, Jabez shifted his future by refusing to accept the name "sorrow" placed on him (1 Chronicles 4:9–10). He cried out for blessing and expansion—and God granted it.

4. YOUR WORDS CAN BIRTH OR BURY A MIRACLE

You can pray fervently, but then cancel it with doubt through your speech.

- "I believe God will heal me . . ." → followed by: "But I never seem to get better . . ."
- "God will provide . . ." → followed by: "I'm always broke . . ."

Your mouth must agree with your faith.

5. SPEAK LIFE DAILY

- Say what God says about you: "I am fearfully and wonderfully made."
- Speak into your destiny: "I am called, equipped, and anointed."
- Declare the promises of God: "All things are working together for my good."

Make your words a launching pad, not a landing strip.

REFLECTION

1. What are you saying about yourself today?
2. Are your words aligned with God's promises or with your fears?
3. Do your words reflect a heart full of faith or full of frustration?

PRAYER

Father, thank You for the creative power You have placed in my tongue. Help me to speak life, truth, and hope over every situation. Let my words reflect Your heart, not my fear. Guard my tongue from careless speech, and fill my mouth with declarations of faith. Let every word I speak build Your Kingdom—in me and through me. In Jesus' name. Amen.

95

A Life of Encouragement and Humility

"Joseph, a Levite from Cyprus, whom the apostles called Barnabas (which means 'son of encouragement'), sold a field he owned and brought the money and put it at the apostles' feet" (Acts 4:36–37).

In a world obsessed with being first, being famous, and being followed, Barnabas offers us a countercultural model of leadership: the power of quiet encouragement, humble service, and generous support. His life was not marked by fame, but by fruit. He was not the loudest voice in the room, but often the most life-giving.

1. BARNABAS THE ENCOURAGER

Barnabas wasn't just given a name—he was given a reputation.

He was known as the "son of encouragement." He made it his mission to lift others—especially the broken, the doubted, and the emerging.

Encouragement isn't just words—it's a lifestyle.

It is intentionally investing in people when they are overlooked or underestimated.

2. HE WAS GENEROUS (ACTS 4:36–37)

Barnabas gave from his resources without being asked, fueling the mission of the early church.

His giving wasn't transactional—it was transformational.

Real encouragement costs something. It involves time, resources, and heart.

3. HE INVESTED IN THE OUTCAST

When Saul (later Paul) was still feared by the church, Barnabas took a risk on him (Acts 9:26–27). He believed in the potential others couldn't see yet.

Encouragers see beyond history and into destiny.

They give people a second chance to walk into God's purpose.

4. HE WAS WILLING TO SERVE IN THE SHADOWS

Though Barnabas initially led alongside Paul, he later took a supporting role. He didn't resist it. He didn't resent it. He rejoiced.

A secure heart doesn't mind when others rise.

You can be great without being first.

5. HE COULD CELEBRATE OTHERS' VICTORIES

Barnabas was never threatened by Paul's growing influence or gifting. He had no agenda, no insecurity.

You know you're growing in maturity when someone else's promotion doesn't feel like your rejection.

6. HE HAD NOTHING TO PROVE, NOTHING TO LOSE

Barnabas lived from a place of security in God. He wasn't caught up in comparison or competition. He simply wanted to serve well and finish well.

REFLECTION

1. Who are you encouraging today?
2. Are you able to celebrate others' growth without comparison?
3. Are you willing to invest in someone others have written off?

PRAYER

Lord, make me an encourager like Barnabas. Help me see the potential in others and invest in them without fear or pride. Teach me to celebrate the victories of others and to live with nothing to prove and nothing to lose. May my life reflect humility, generosity, and Christlike love. In Jesus' name. Amen.

96

When Life Feels Out of Control

"When he saw Jesus, he cried out and fell at his feet, shouting at the top of his voice, 'What do you want with me, Jesus, Son of the Most High God? I beg you, don't torture me!'" (Luke 8:28).

Life can unravel in ways that leave us feeling out of control—emotionally, mentally, spiritually. In Luke 8, we meet a man tormented by demons, living in isolation, harming himself, and unable to be restrained by society. Yet in this darkest of places, Jesus shows up—not to condemn, but to confront and deliver.

1. LIVING IN ISOLATION

Isolation is one of Satan's most effective tactics. The enemy knows that if he can separate you from community and silence your voice, he can torment you without resistance.

The man in Luke 8 lived among tombs—disconnected, shamed, and forgotten.

But Jesus crossed a stormy sea just to reach that one broken soul.

You may feel alone, but you are not abandoned. Jesus always comes to find you.

2. OUT OF CONTROL AND SELF-DESTRUCTIVE

The demoniac's behavior was self-harming and chaotic. That's what lasciviousness looks like: the inability to control appetites, urges, or emotions. It's bondage masquerading as freedom.

Sin promises relief but delivers ruin.

The man didn't need more rules—he needed deliverance.

3. DELIVERANCE BEGINS WITH A CRY

When the man saw Jesus, he cried out and fell down before Him. Even the demons within him recognized authority and had to bow.

There is always a collision between darkness and the light of Christ. In that collision, Jesus doesn't flinch—He commands peace.

Your freedom begins when you stop resisting and start surrendering.

4. JESUS CONFRONTS WHAT CONTROLS YOU

"For this purpose the Son of God was manifested, that He might destroy the works of the devil" (1 John 3:8).

Jesus did not come to manage your mess—He came to demolish it. Whether it's fear, addiction, anger, or shame, when Jesus steps in, the stronghold must bow.

5. RESTORATION IS THE GOAL

After his deliverance, the man was found:
- Clothed.
- In his right mind.
- Sitting at the feet of Jesus.

That's the picture of restoration. Jesus brings not only freedom from sin, but also dignity, identity, and peace.

REFLECTION

1. Are there areas of your life that feel out of control right now?
2. Have you isolated yourself from the very people who could help you heal?
3. What needs to bow to the Lordship of Jesus in your life today?

PRAYER

Jesus, You see me even when I feel lost, ashamed, or overwhelmed. Come and confront the chaos in my heart. Speak peace to the storm within me. I surrender everything that has bound me—fear, shame, addiction, pride—and I invite Your deliverance. Restore my mind, my soul, and my identity. Help me live loved, even when life feels out of control. In Your name. Amen.

97

Trusting God in Impossible Situations

"But Jesus looked at them and said to them, 'With man this is impossible, but with God all things are possible'" (Matthew 19:26).

Life often presents us with situations that feel unmovable, unchangeable, and downright impossible. Whether it's a health crisis, a broken relationship, or a dead-end dream, we've all encountered moments where human strength isn't enough. But the good news of the Gospel is this: God is not limited by what limits us.

Jehoshaphat, in 2 Chronicles 20, gives us a blueprint for navigating the impossible. His nation was under threat by a vast army, but instead of reacting in fear, he chose to respond in faith.

1. SEEK GOD IN PRAYER AND FASTING

"Jehoshaphat feared and set himself to seek the LORD . . ." (2 Chronicles 20:3).

When the battle looms, don't panic—pray. Fasting and prayer shift our focus from fear to faith, from problems to the presence of God.

What you turn to in crisis reveals what you trust.

2. SURROUND YOURSELF WITH FAITH PEOPLE

Not everyone is equipped to stand with you in battle.
- Flesh people magnify fear.
- Faith people magnify God.

Surround yourself with those who will speak truth, stand in prayer, and remind you of who God is—even when the odds seem impossible.

3. STAND ON GOD'S PROMISES

Jehoshaphat prayed: "Are You not God in heaven? And do You not rule over all the kingdoms . . . ?" He wasn't reminding God—he was reminding himself.

Don't let the size of your problem make you forget the power of your God.

4. FOLLOW GOD'S INSTRUCTIONS

"Do not be afraid nor dismayed . . . for the battle is not yours, but God's" (2 Chronicles 20:15).

God's strategies often don't make sense to the natural mind. But miracles are born through obedience, not logic.

You don't need to know how God will do it—just listen and obey.

5. KNOW YOUR PLACE IN THE BATTLE

"Position yourselves, stand still, and see the salvation of the Lord."

There are times God says fight, and times He says stand still. Knowing the difference is key.

Faith sometimes looks like movement, and sometimes like rest.

6. PRAISE GOD IN THE BATTLE

Jehoshaphat sent worshippers ahead of the army. Their praise confused the enemy and triggered victory.

Praise is your weapon. Worship is your warfare.

7. HONOR GOD AFTER THE BREAKTHROUGH

Don't forget the God who brought you through. Let your deliverance become a testimony that strengthens others and gives God the glory.

REFLECTION

1. What "impossible" situation are you facing today?
2. Have you brought it to God in prayer and positioned yourself in faith?
3. Are you surrounding yourself with faith people or flesh people?

PRAYER

Lord, I acknowledge that there are things I cannot fix, control, or overcome on my own. But You are the God of the impossible. Teach me to seek You, stand on Your promises, follow Your instructions, and praise You—even before I see the breakthrough. I trust You with the battle, knowing the victory belongs to You. In Jesus' name. Amen.

98

God's Way to Make Decisions

"Trust in the LORD with all your heart and lean not on your own understanding; in all your ways acknowledge Him, and He shall direct your paths" (Proverbs 3:5–6, NKJV).

We all face moments when we need to make decisions—some small, others life-altering. The challenge is not just about choosing something but about choosing wisely and God's way. The Bible gives us a divine framework for navigating the unknown with clarity, peace, and faith.

1. START WITH PRAYER AND THE WORD

Every godly decision begins with a posture of seeking. Before you talk to others, talk to God. Invite His direction, and search His Word. Many answers are already found in Scripture—either through direct commands, examples, or principles.

God's will is never inconsistent with God's Word.

2. LISTEN FOR THE WHISPER

The Holy Spirit is our Counselor and Guide. While the world screams, the Spirit whispers.

Learn to discern His voice through quiet reflection, worship, and spiritual sensitivity.

"My sheep hear My voice . . ." (John 10:27).

Clarity comes in the stillness, not the chaos.

3. SEEK GODLY COUNSEL

We are not meant to decide in isolation. Wise voices around us provide safety.

"In the multitude of counselors there is safety" (Proverbs 11:14).

Find people who know God's Word and aren't afraid to tell you the truth—even when it's uncomfortable.

4. ASK THE RIGHT QUESTIONS

For decisions that aren't clearly right or wrong, apply biblical principles:
- Does it glorify God? (1 Corinthians 10:31)
- What is my motive? (James 4:3)
- Is it beneficial or just permissible? (1 Corinthians 6:12)
- Will it promote spiritual growth—or hinder it? (Mark 4:19)
- Could this enslave me or become a habit? (John 8:34)
- Will this compromise my witness? (2 Corinthians 6:14)
- Does it lead me closer to temptation or away from it? (James 1:13–15)
- Does it give the appearance of evil? (1 Thessalonians 5:22)
- How will it affect others? Will it edify? (Romans 14:19)

God doesn't just care about what you decide, but why and how.

5. WAIT ON PEACE

If your spirit feels unsettled, wait. God's will is often marked by peace, not pressure.

"Let the peace of Christ rule in your hearts . . ." (Colossians 3:15).

If there's no peace, there's no release. Don't move just because you're tired of waiting.

6. WALK BY FAITH, NOT BY FEAR

Sometimes the right decision still feels risky. But God rarely leads us into comfort—He leads us into obedience.

If you're walking in faith, it won't always feel safe—but it will always be right.

REFLECTION

1. What decision are you facing right now?
2. Are you leaning on your own understanding or seeking God's?

3. Have you invited the Holy Spirit, Scripture, and godly counsel into the process?

PRAYER

Lord, I surrender my decisions to You. Lead me in Your truth and teach me to walk in wisdom. Help me not to lean on my own understanding but to seek Your voice, Your Word, and Your peace. May my choices reflect Your heart, bring You glory, and edify those around me. In Jesus' name. Amen.

99

God's Got You

"The LORD your God is with you, the Mighty Warrior who saves. He will take great delight in you; in His love He will no longer rebuke you, but will rejoice over you with singing" (Zephaniah 3:17).

Life has a way of making us feel vulnerable, inadequate, and even forgotten. Whether you're walking through uncertainty, grief, failure, or fear—this truth stands firm: God's got you. He is with you, for you, and ahead of you in all things.

1. GOD IS FAITHFUL EVEN WHEN WE ARE NOT

We often stumble. We doubt, get discouraged, or even turn away for a season. But God's faithfulness is not built on our performance—it's grounded in His character.

"If we are unfaithful, He remains faithful, for He cannot deny who He is" (2 Timothy 2:13, NLT).

Your mistakes don't disqualify you from His mercy. You are still held by the One whose love never fails.

2. GOD STRENGTHENS THE WEAK

Throughout Scripture, God used people with limitations:
- Moses had a speech issue.
- Gideon felt like a nobody.
- Hannah lived with unanswered prayers.
- Peter denied Christ—but was restored.

God doesn't require perfection. He gives strength for the battle, courage for the valley, and grace for every new day.

"He gives power to the weak and strength to the powerless" (Isaiah 40:29, NLT).

3. GOD PROTECTS YOU FROM THE EVIL ONE

This world is full of temptation, distraction, and spiritual attacks. But Jesus prayed for us to be kept from the evil one (John 17:15), and taught us to do the same (Matthew 6:13).

You are not unguarded. God watches over your going out and coming in (Psalm 121).

His protection is not just physical, but spiritual, emotional, and eternal.

4. GOD REJOICES OVER YOU

It's hard to imagine, but true—God doesn't just tolerate you; He delights in you. He rejoices over you with singing (Zephaniah 3:17). His love is not passive; it is pursuing, powerful, and personal.

He doesn't just rescue you—He rejoices over you.

REFLECTION

1. Are you trusting God's faithfulness or your own feelings?
2. What area of weakness do you need His strength for today?
3. Do you believe God is protecting and watching over your life?

PRAYER

Lord, thank You that You are faithful, even when I am not. Thank You that Your strength meets me in my weakness, and Your protection surrounds me in every battle. Help me to rest in the truth that You've got me—fully, completely, and always. I place my trust in You today. In Jesus' name. Amen.

100

Invest in Souls: The Eternal Value of a Life

"For what shall it profit a man, if he shall gain the whole world, and lose his own soul?" (Mark 8:36, KJV).

In a world that places high value on possessions, prestige, and power, Jesus reminds us of something eternally true: Nothing is more valuable than a soul. Not a mansion. Not a billion-dollar yacht. Not even the entire world. Souls are priceless because they are eternal, created by God, and redeemed by Christ.

1. THE SOUL IS GOD-BREATHED AND ETERNAL

Genesis 2:7 says God breathed life into man, and he became a living soul. Unlike possessions, which fade, a soul returns to God (Ecclesiastes 12:7). Your soul is the only eternal part of you—and it's the only thing that truly belongs to you.

What we see is temporary. What we invest in souls impacts eternity.

2. THE COST OF A SOUL IS BEYOND MEASURE

First Peter 1:18–19 tells us we were not redeemed with silver or gold, but with the precious blood of Jesus Christ. The value of something is often measured by what someone is willing to pay for it—and God paid for each soul with the life of His Son.

That alone reveals the infinite worth of every person you meet.

3. WHY SHOULD WE INVEST IN SOULS?

1. It is wise. "He who wins souls is wise" (Proverbs 11:30).
2. Every soul can be transformed into Christ's likeness.

3. Eternal consequences: a lost soul is forever separated from God (Matthew 25:46).
4. There is a reward in this life and in the life to come (Mark 10:29–30).

Investing in souls is not just an act of compassion—it's an act of wisdom, obedience, and worship.

4. WHAT CAN WE INVEST?
- Time – Be present, listen, mentor, disciple.
- Talents – Use your gifts to build up others.
- Treasure – Support missions, outreach, and ministries that lead people to Christ.

You don't need to have everything. You just need to offer what's in your hands (Exodus 4:2).

5. HOW DO WE INVEST?
- PLAN diligently – "The plans of the diligent lead to abundance . . ." (Proverbs 21:5).
- VISION – Ask God to show you where and whom to serve.
- DREAM – What has God placed in your heart? Big dreams begin with small steps.

Eternal investments begin with present obedience.

REFLECTION
1. Whose soul is God placing on your heart right now?
2. Are you prioritizing eternal investments over temporary gain?
3. What is in your hands today that God wants to use?

PRAYER

Father, thank You for reminding me of what truly matters. Help me to see people the way You do—full of worth and eternal purpose. Teach me to invest my time, talents, and treasure in what cannot be lost. Break my heart for the lost and give me the courage to love, serve, and speak truth. Let my life count for eternity. In Jesus' name. Amen.

Extra Gold Mine Nuggets to Enrich Your Life

101

Begin with the End in Mind

"Let your eyes look straight ahead; fix your gaze directly before you" (Proverbs 4:25).

In a culture driven by busyness and distraction, we are constantly doing more, moving faster, and accomplishing less that truly matters. The question isn't, are you active? But, are you focused? As believers, we are called to live with the end in mind—the eternal end, God's purpose for our lives, and the legacy we leave behind.

1. SEE THE END BEFORE YOU START

Stephen Covey once wrote, "Begin with the end in mind." God calls us to do the same. Abraham was told to "lift up your eyes and look . . ." (Genesis 13:14–15). God gave him a vision before He gave him direction.

If we don't know where we're going, we'll waste time on what doesn't matter.

Vision informs purpose. Purpose shapes priorities.

2. PURPOSE LEADS TO CLARITY

Paul said, "This one thing I do . . ." (Philippians 3:13). He had a laser focus, shaped by his divine calling. Likewise, you and I must ask: What is the one thing God has called me to do in this season? Without clarity, we get caught in distraction, doing a hundred things poorly instead of one thing well.

Knowing your purpose allows you to say yes to what matters and no to what doesn't.

3. FAITH REQUIRES IMAGINATION

Covey noted that all things are created twice: first in the mind, then in reality. Likewise, faith envisions what is not yet visible. Hebrews 11:1 says faith is "the substance of things hoped for." Faith-filled vision is about seeing through the eyes of the Spirit, not the limits of circumstance.

God's promises are often received in the spirit first—before they ever show up in the natural.

4. BE INTENTIONAL, NOT ACCIDENTAL

Like the Cheshire Cat told Alice in Wonderland: "If you don't know where you want to go, then it doesn't matter which way you go."

Without intentionality, you'll live by default instead of by design.

God doesn't want you to drift—He wants you to walk purposefully in His will, planning your steps with Him (Proverbs 16:9).

5. KINGDOM VISION BUILDS THE CHURCH

When we begin with God's ultimate end in mind—the Great Commission—we see that investing in souls, church planting, and leadership training become eternally significant. Global Church Network, founded by Dr. James O. Davis' mission to mobilize leaders, reflects this vision: to plant churches, train planters, and reach the unreached.

God's endgame is a harvest of souls. And He's chosen you to help gather it.

REFLECTION

1. Have you been busy, but directionless?
2. What "end" is shaping your current life decisions?
3. What is your "one thing" God is calling you to focus on today?

PRAYER

Lord, give me eyes to see with eternity in mind. Remove every distraction that keeps me from pursuing Your purpose. Help me to fix my eyes on You and walk boldly in the vision You've given. Let my life be shaped by what matters most—Your Kingdom, Your people, and Your glory. In Jesus' name. Amen.

102

Finding Strength in the Secret Place

"Why, my soul, are you downcast? Why so disturbed within me? Put your hope in God, for I will yet praise him, my Savior and my God" (Psalm 42:11).

Discouragement is one of the enemy's most subtle and destructive weapons. It creeps in silently, fueled by disappointment, unmet expectations, and comparison. It drains our joy, clouds our vision, and causes us to question our worth and calling. As believers, we are not immune to discouragement—but we are not powerless against it.

1. RECOGNIZE THE SIGNS

Like Hannah in 1 Samuel 1, we may find ourselves overwhelmed with tears, downhearted, and in anguish. Discouragement often appears as:

- Loneliness
- Weariness
- Restlessness
- Heaviness
- Helplessness

These emotional weights can lead us to withdraw, question our purpose, or even become bitter.

Don't ignore discouragement—acknowledge it, but don't let it define you.

2. IDENTIFY THE ROOT CAUSES

Discouragement often stems from:

- Negative voices.
- Unrealistic expectations.
- Lack of recognition.
- Comparing ourselves to others.
- Feeling alone in the struggle.
- Personal failure or delayed breakthrough.

The enemy often lies to us when we're tired, alone, or under pressure.

You are not failing—you are facing a battle.

3. REMEMBER: IT'S TEMPORARY

Even the strongest people of faith—Elijah, David, Hannah—faced discouragement. But it didn't last forever.

"Weeping may endure for a night, but joy comes in the morning" (Psalm 30:5).

Discouragement is a moment, not your identity.

4. ENDURE AND EMBRACE PURPOSE

Second Timothy 2:3 reminds us: "Endure hardship as a good soldier of Christ."

Your current struggle may feel like a detour, but it's part of God's divine design. Romans 8:28 assures us that God uses everything—even our pain—for purpose.

Purpose doesn't erase pain, but it gives it meaning.

5. DWELL IN THE SECRET PLACE

Your strength is restored in God's presence. Don't let discouragement drive you away from God—let it draw you into the secret place. It's where clarity returns and peace is restored.

6. ENCOURAGE YOURSELF IN THE LORD

Ephesians 5:19 teaches us to "speak to yourselves in psalms and hymns . . ."

David encouraged himself when no one else could. Sometimes the best sermon you'll ever hear is the one you preach to your own heart.

Open your mouth. Speak truth. Sing worship. Shift the atmosphere.

REFLECTION
1. What is currently weighing on your heart?
2. Have you been trying to carry it alone?
3. How can you encourage yourself in God today?

PRAYER

Father, I admit that I feel discouraged. I'm weary, and sometimes I struggle to see what You're doing. But I choose today to place my hope in You. I believe this season is not the end of the story. Teach me to endure, to dwell in Your presence, and to find joy in the secret place. Strengthen me to encourage myself in You and keep my eyes fixed on the greater purpose. In Jesus' name. Amen.

103

Strength in the Storm

"But He said to me, 'My grace is sufficient for you, for My power is made perfect in weakness.' Therefore I will boast all the more gladly about my weaknesses, so that Christ's power may rest on me" (2 Corinthians 12:9).

Suffering has a way of stripping us down to what truly matters. It disrupts our comfort, exposes our weakness, and confronts our theology. Like Paul, we may ask: "Why God? What is happening to me? Where are You in the middle of this pain?" The truth is—you are not alone, and God is still at work.

1. EVERYONE FACES SUFFERING

Whether it's sickness, sorrow, or struggle, suffering touches every life. You are either:

- In the middle of a storm.
- Coming out of one.
- Or about to sail into one.

No one escapes pain in this fallen world. But God promises to meet us in our weakness, not only on the other side of it.

2. GOD IS WORKING THROUGH IT

Paul's "thorn in the flesh" was a constant, painful reminder of his humanity. But it also became the stage upon which God's power was most clearly displayed.

The suffering didn't go away—but grace showed up in greater measure.

Suffering + Grace = Strength

3. GOD SPEAKS IN OUR SUFFERING

Paul pleaded three times for the thorn to be removed. But instead of removal, God gave a revelation: "My grace is sufficient for you."

God may not always change your situation—but He will use it to change you.

His presence is bigger than your problems.

His purpose is greater than your pain.

4. HOW YOU RESPOND MATTERS

Suffering can produce two very different responses:

- Resistance, resentment, and bitterness → defeat
- Prayerfulness, faith, and trust → victory

You can't always choose your circumstances, but you can choose your posture.

When we embrace our weakness, Christ's power rests on us.

REFLECTION

- What storm are you currently walking through?
- Have you asked God to remove something instead of receiving His grace in it?
- Are you responding with faith—or with frustration?

PRAYER

Father, I don't always understand the pain I face, but I choose to trust You. Teach me to lean into Your grace when life feels unbearable. Let my weakness become a doorway for Your strength to shine through. I release resentment and embrace Your purpose, knowing You are working in me—even now. In Jesus' name. Amen.

104

A Fresh Start

"Jesus replied, 'Very truly I tell you, no one can see the kingdom of God unless they are born again'" (John 3:3).

There are moments in life when all we long for is a do-over—a second chance, a clean slate, a fresh beginning. Whether it's a failed plan, a broken heart, or just the weight of trying to live right and still falling short, the cry is the same: "Can I start over?"

The answer from Jesus is clear: Yes. But it starts with being born again.

1. THE SEARCH FOR A NEW BEGINNING

Nicodemus came to Jesus under the cover of night—curious, hungry, maybe even desperate. A respected religious leader, yet still empty inside. He had rules, but no rest; knowledge, but no newness.

Even religion can leave you dry if it lacks relationship.

Jesus saw right through the formality and offered him not more rules, but rebirth.

2. WHAT IT MEANS TO BE BORN AGAIN

Jesus explained that new life doesn't come through effort, status, or trying harder.

It comes by being born of water and of the Spirit (John 3:5).

- Water symbolizes cleansing, repentance, and baptism—a turning from the old.
- Spirit points to divine regeneration—a supernatural act of God, not man.

The new birth isn't self-improvement. It's a spiritual resurrection.

3. WHY WE ALL NEED A FRESH START

Nicodemus needed to be freed from religious baggage. Many of us need to be freed from:

- Shame from past mistakes.
- The crushing weight of expectations..
- Regret over missed opportunities.
- Emotional or spiritual numbness.

You can't walk in new life while wearing the grave clothes of your past.

4. JESUS IS IN THE FRESH START BUSINESS

God is not just the God of second chances—He's the God of new creations.

As Job once cried out, "My days are past . . . my plans are shattered . . ." (Job 17:11).

But Jesus steps in to restore what's broken and give us a new purpose.

5. THE KINGDOM AWAITS

Jesus said unless a man is born again, he cannot see or enter the Kingdom of God.

A fresh start is not only about peace here—it's about entering the life God has always intended for you.

REFLECTION

1. Are you trying to start over without surrendering fully to Jesus?
2. What "old coat" do you need to lay down at the door of grace?
3. Have you experienced the spiritual rebirth Jesus offers?

PRAYER

Lord, I long for a fresh start. I bring You my mistakes, my regrets, and the broken pieces of my story. Thank You for offering me new birth, not based on what I've done, but on who You are. I receive Your love, Your cleansing, and Your Spirit. Make me new, Lord. Today, I start again—with You. In Jesus' name. Amen.

105

What Are You Willing to Give?

"And when He had finished speaking, He said to Simon, 'Put out into deep water, and let down the nets for a catch.' Simon answered, 'Master, we've worked hard all night and haven't caught anything. But because you say so, I will let down the nets'" (Luke 5:4–5).

Sometimes God doesn't ask us to do something convenient—He asks us to do something costly. In Luke 5, Jesus borrows Peter's boat, uses it as a platform to teach, and then calls Peter to "launch out into the deep." It wasn't just a fishing trip. It was a moment of decision—a divine invitation. The question is: What are you willing to give when God calls?

1. GIVING WHAT'S IN YOUR HAND

Peter didn't give what he didn't have. He gave what was available—his boat, his time, and his trust. Though exhausted and empty-handed after a night of failure, Peter still responded to Jesus' request.

God often asks for what you already have—not for what you think you need first.

2. OBEDIENCE BEYOND LOGIC

Peter had every reason to say no:
- He was tired.
- He had already tried and failed.
- He was washing his nets, signaling closure for the day.

But Peter didn't follow his own reasoning—he obeyed "at Your word." That's faith.

Obedience doesn't always make sense, but it always bears fruit when rooted in trust.

3. EXCUSES VS. OBEDIENCE

Peter could have offered valid excuses:
- "We already tried."
- "It's not the right time."
- "We're fishermen—we know this lake."

But instead, he surrendered his expertise to the word of Christ.

The more you trust your excuses, the more you limit your encounter.

4. GOD USES WHAT YOU GIVE TO BLESS OTHERS

Peter's willingness didn't just bless him—it impacted everyone around him. The catch was so large that the nets began to break, and other boats were called to help. When you give sacrificially to God, the blessing overflows.

What you give in faith becomes a miracle in God's hands.

5. A SHIFT IN PURPOSE

After the miracle, Peter recognized Jesus not just as a teacher, but as Lord. And Jesus didn't stop there—He called Peter to a new purpose: "From now on you will fish for people" (Luke 5:10).

Giving what you have now can unlock who you are meant to become.

REFLECTION

1. What is God asking you to give today? Time? Trust? Resources? Obedience?
2. Are you offering excuses or stepping forward in faith?
3. How might your act of giving become a blessing for others?

PRAYER

Lord, help me to surrender what I have, even when I feel tired, unsure, or inadequate. Teach me to trust Your word above my circumstances. Use my small offering as a platform for Your glory. Let my obedience lead to blessing—not just for me, but for those around me. In Jesus' name. Amen.

TRUTH TO HOLD

God doesn't ask for what's perfect—He asks for what's available. When you give Him your boat, He'll fill your nets—and then call you to a greater purpose.

106

Freedom from the Trap of Offense

"It is impossible but that offences will come: but woe unto him, through whom they come!" (Luke 17:1, KJV).

Offense is one of Satan's most effective weapons to divide, distract, and ultimately destroy. Jesus Himself warned us that offenses are inevitable—but how we respond determines whether we fall into bondage or walk in freedom.

1. OFFENSE IS SATAN'S TRAP

In 2 Timothy 2:26, Paul describes offense as a snare of the devil, capturing people to do his will. When we allow bitterness to fester, we become spiritually trapped—taken captive by the enemy's strategy of division and deception.

Offense is the bait. Pride is the hook. Bitterness is the chain.

2. THE DEVASTATING FRUIT OF OFFENSE

When left unresolved, offense produces:
- Hurt
- Anger
- Resentment
- Bitterness
- Jealousy
- Outrage

These fruits blind us to our true spiritual condition and keep us inward-focused and defensive.

A heart poisoned by offense loses its capacity to love unconditionally.

3. WHAT OFFENSE ROBS YOU OF . . .
- **Purpose:** Offense derails your calling and steals your joy (Ecclesiastes 10:4).
- **Peace:** Psalm 119:165 says, "Great peace have they which love thy law: and nothing shall offend them."
- **Perspective:** Offense clouds judgment and keeps us focused on self instead of Christ.

Offense magnifies the wound and minimizes grace.

4. HEALING BEGINS WITH FORGIVENESS

Forgiveness is not about letting someone off the hook—it's about setting yourself free. John 20:23 reminds us that forgiveness is a reflection of the heart. Holding back forgiveness often comes from a sense of being treated unjustly, but forgiveness releases both you and the offender.

Forgiveness is not a feeling—it's a decision fueled by grace.

5. SEEING CLEARLY AGAIN

Revelation 3:18 calls us to anoint our eyes so we may see again. Offense blinds us, but God offers healing clarity through repentance, surrender, and love.

REFLECTION
1. Is there an offense you've been carrying that's clouding your heart?
2. Are you willing to forgive, even if the other person never apologizes?
3. What would it look like for you to love unconditionally today?

PRAYER

Father, I confess that I've allowed offense to take root in my heart. I lay down the right to be angry, to be bitter, or to retaliate. I choose forgiveness—not because they deserve it, but because You forgave me. Heal my heart, restore my peace, and help me walk in the freedom of love unconditionally. In Jesus' name. Amen.

107

When People Try to Hurt You

"But I prayed, 'Now strengthen my hands'" (Nehemiah 6:9).

Have you ever faced betrayal by someone close? Have you ever been falsely accused, misunderstood, or attacked while simply trying to do what's right? Nehemiah knew what that felt like. He wasn't doing something wrong—he was doing something great for God. And yet, that's exactly when the opposition rose up.

1. THE ENEMY IS SUBTLE

Sanballat and his crew weren't obvious at first. They acted like they had Nehemiah's best interest at heart: "Come, let us meet together . . ." (Nehemiah 6:2). But Nehemiah discerned the truth—they were plotting to harm him.

Not everyone who smiles at you is for you.

The enemy often disguises harm as concern.

2. THE TACTIC OF INTIMIDATION

When subtlety failed, the enemy used pressure and public accusation. They wrote open letters full of lies to provoke fear:

"You are planning to revolt . . . You want to be king . . ." (Nehemiah 6:6–7).

But Nehemiah refused to panic or run. He saw the tactic for what it was: fear meant to stop the work.

When people try to hurt you, it's often a distraction to weaken your hands and delay your purpose.

3. NEHEMIAH'S BOLD RESPONSE

Nehemiah didn't cower or retaliate. He simply replied:

"Nothing like what you are saying is happening; you are just making it up out of your head" (Nehemiah 6:8).

Then he turned to God: "Now strengthen my hands" (Nehemiah 6:9).

When people try to tear you down, don't fight back in the flesh—fight on your knees.

4. DISCERN FALSE PROPHETS AND MANIPULATION

Even religious voices tried to intimidate Nehemiah—using fear and false prophecy to make him retreat. But Nehemiah had spiritual discernment. He realized:

"God had not sent him . . . He had been hired to intimidate me . . ." (Nehemiah 6:12–13).

Not every "spiritual word" is from God. Test every voice by His truth.

5. HOW TO RESPOND WHEN PEOPLE TRY TO HURT YOU

- Stay focused on the mission God gave you. "I am doing a great work and cannot come down" (Nehemiah 6:3).
- Don't retaliate. Let God expose motives in time (1 Peter 2:12,15).
- Be bold, not bitter. Refuse to act out of fear or pride.
- Pray for strength, not revenge.
- Trust God to be your defender.

REFLECTION

1. Are you being distracted or discouraged by someone's false words?
2. Are you tempted to respond in the flesh or run in fear?
3. Can you pray like Nehemiah, "Lord, strengthen my hands"?

PRAYER

Lord, when people try to hurt me, remind me that my identity is secure in You. Teach me not to fight back with my words but to fight forward in prayer. Give me discernment to see what's true, courage to stand firm, and faith to trust You as my Defender. Strengthen my hands to keep doing the work You've called me to do. In Jesus' name. Amen.

A Final Word to the Reader

Dear Friend,

If this book has stirred your heart, challenged your habits, or drawn you closer to Jesus, then my prayer has been answered. These pages were never meant to point to me, but to the One who called me—the Lord who redeems our stories and reshapes our lives through His grace.

I have learned that discipline is not about striving in our own strength, but about staying surrendered to His. Each step of obedience, no matter how small, becomes sacred when it is offered to God in faith.

My encouragement to you is simple: keep growing. Keep showing up in prayer, keep opening God's Word, keep loving people well, and keep choosing integrity even when no one sees. Over time, you'll look back and realize that the Spirit of God has been forming something beautiful in you—the character of Christ.

Thank you for allowing me to walk with you through these reflections. May the wisdom of God steady your heart, may His Spirit strengthen your resolve, and may His grace carry you into a life of lasting fruitfulness.

With love and faith,
Ejaz Nabie

www.ingramcontent.com/pod-product-compliance
Lightning Source LLC
Chambersburg PA
CBHW032038150426
43194CB00006B/331